*A BOOK THAT REMOVES ALL LABELS AND EN-ABLES ALL INDIVIDUALS TO BE AS ONE COLLECTIVE SPIRIT*

"Each person must travel their own destiny journey. This journey (whether short or long term), has in its grasp a compass. This compass, if adhered to, will safely guide the traveler successfully through various terrains of life. Check Your Life: Be Limitless, The Power Behind the Words by Dr. James Williams, is a life and business compass. It has been meticulously inscribed by a prolific scholar, with research, wisdom and a breadth experience. Discover helpful insights towards excavating your truest potential! As someone who have known Dr. Williams personally, I have not only seen him go from Thug to Scholar but have witnessed tangible evidence of the success principals he has placed in this book. I would encourage any person at any point of their life to add this book to their library—referring to it as often as possible!"

**Savaslas Lofton, MBA**
*Leadership, Marketing & Author of At a Mirror's Glance and Letting Go of the Perfect*

"*Check Your Life: Be Limitless* – creates a space for us to let go of fear and move toward a life that embraces our truest self. By digging deep into the core of who we are by answering the questions in this book, only helps to create stronger, more meaningful relationships. We are allowed to let go of our self-judgement and in-

i

stead, fill our minds and hearts with love, courage, patience, and creativity. Taking time to truly reflect and question the world around us allows for a deeper, more meaningful existence. Will you embark on this journey to unmask your true potential?"
*Stefanie Benjamin, PhD – Assistant Professor and Co-Director of Tourism RESET*

"James Arthur Williams has combined his awareness of many beautiful traditions to reach a point of self awareness; where one can let go of the assigned roles, our masks, and many more limiting beliefs in our life with a series of checks. Through these checks, we can find and experience our authenticity, which is a limitless life. With creativity and awareness, this book will help you along your own journey towards healing and unconditional love."
*Don Miguel Ruiz Jr.*
*Author of The Five Levels of Attachment*
*The Mastery of Self*
*Living a Life of Awareness*

"Every once in a while a book comes out, that will challenge your beliefs positively and empower you to grow and get better. "Check your Life" is a book, everyone should read more than once! In a provocative and honest manner, the author explores what it really takes to live a courageous and fulfilling life. Filled with stories and personal examples, the book is a pleasant read that will change something in you."
*Stoyan Yankov, Productivity Coach, Professional Speaker and Co-Author of PERFORM, The Unsexy Truth about (Startup) Success*

"James took a story that almost everyone will know and pulls many life lessons. Despite the story coming from the bible, it is a story that has broad applications regardless of the religious beliefs of the reader. The lessons are about how many of our assumptions about ourselves are self-imposed restrictions to living our best life. You think you are not capable of something? James challenges us to ask "says who?" and to instead check your life and remove your self-imposed limitations. He shared some of his life story in order to connect with where he was, where he is, and where he plans to be in the future by living each day to the best of his ability and to continue to exceed high expectations that were set by his former self. This book is set up to take you from the start – where you identify your limits – to the point where you are living each day without restrictions or limits, or as James says – being limitless."

*Eric Brown, PhD - Associate Professor*
*Leadership Expert*


"*Check Your Life* makes you question many areas of your life and opens your mind to thinking beyond what you've been taught and believed for many years. It makes you explore the world and humans beyond labels that we've been given, to open the door to true unconditional love for yourself and everyone you come in contact with. Go on this uncomfortable journey to allow yourself the opportunity to become truly comfortable with yourself and everything and everybody around you."

*La-Toya Williams, MEd - Professional Development Specialist and Former USAF Veteran*


"This is a transformational read that will add value to anyone's journey to better understand themselves and the world around us. The ideas presented are complex but accompanied by examples and storytelling that make them digestible and unintimidating. Each chapter begins with compelling and thought-provoking quotes that create a foundation for the information to come. Dr. Williams has created a true masterpiece that will speak to readers across all de-mographics. Highly recommend!"

*Miranda Kitterlin, PhD - Associate Professor*
*Associate Editor, International Hospitality Review & Coca Cola*
*Endowed Professor*

CHECK YOUR LIFE

# CHECK YOUR LIFE

## *Be Limitless: The Power Behind the Words*

DR. JAMES ARTHUR WILLIAMS

UnmaskYTP Publishing

UNMASKYTP PUBLISHING

For information, please visit our website
*www.unmaskytp.us2.authorhomepage.com* or *www.unmaskytp.com*

**Check Your Life**
by Dr. James Arthur Williams

Thanks to God, my wife, kids, parents, brothers, family, and friends for inspiring me to be limitless and to giving my life to inspire others to be limitless! I will continue to live hard, unconditionally love, and be at peace with all of you sentient beings. This book is dedicated to all of you limitless souls, so I implore you all to be better than your best and to be limitless.

# Contents

Check Your Life: Be Limitless
The Power Behind the Words

What Does It Feel Like to Live a Life with no Labels?

# Glossary of Important Terms

- **A.N.D.** – Stands for Awareness, No judgment, and Do excellence
- **Assigned roles** – A given title, occupation, or position in the physical realm, such as dad, professor, male, or Black.
- **Authentic voice** – Our inherent gifts and/or purpose of existence prior to any domestication or adopted beliefs.
- **B.A.R.** – The process of **believe, aim, receive** that ascends us above finite possibilities.
- **Check Your Life (CYL)** – An instant evaluation of our present situation, to jolt us into a heightened state of consciousness.
- **Conditional love** – When an individual loves another if they meet set conditions that appease them.
- **Domestication** – A process that causes us to believe in some set of rules, labels, and/or manmade ideals.
- **God/god** – A capitalized God stands for a permanent understanding that the infinite intelligence, omnipresent, or religion-based God always dwells inside us . A lowercased god represents temporary peace, joy, and/or brief moments of understanding that God dwells on the inside.
- **Hero** – An individual who decides to see opportunities in failures or shortcomings and who decides to use those opportunities to overcome those failures.
- **Label** – A name or definition assigned to an object or individual.

- **Lies** – Ideas, opinions, and/or beliefs accepted that oppose our authentic voice or limit our inner Gods.

- **Limitless** – A unification of mind, spirit, and body to believe in achieving the perceived impossible.

- **Loud noise phase** – A time when we are free and do not refer to labels; but then, we are introduced to "no" and many other labels/categories of awareness in our lives. This information is communicated by influencers and impressionable people in our individual worlds.

- **Mask** – An extreme belief into an assigned role to the point that it alters our authentic voice, causing us to adopt our given identity.

- **Physical realm** – A place where our fleshly bodies or physical forms interact with places, things, and other physical forms.

- **Religion** – Manmade or finite being set of rules and practices to serve an infinite spirit or deity.

- **Sentient being** – An individual with consciousness or some deeper context about life itself.

- **Sin** – Any action, belief, or internal saying you commit to harm yourself, mentally or physically.

- **Spiritual realm** – A place of the unseen where esoteric knowledge is hidden, and from which our spirits originate.

- **Tree of knowledge** – A symbolic representation of people eating fruit that labels individuals, places, and things in our shared societies.

- **Tree of life** – A symbolic representation of people eating fruit that is void of labeling in our shared societies.

- **Truth** – Beliefs that enable us to be at peace and to align with our authentic voice.

- **Unconditional love** – When an individual loves another

beyond any set condition, by accepting all their so-called strengths and so-called flaws, without needing another person to appease them.

- **Victim** – An individual who blames others and/or situations for their failures or shortcomings.

# Introduction

*"Discovering the truth about ourselves is a lifetime's work, but it's*
*worth the effort."*
*~ Fred Rogers*

Life is a mystery. This mystery can be experienced with excitement and mystical wonder, or it can be experienced with disdain and boredom. This split-second decision is offered in every conscious, waking moment we have in the physical realm. We consciously (or unconsciously) venture through our individual daily lives, and all of us have worn the victim mask and eaten apples of boredom. Our greatest conundrum is our common, daily desire to eat fruit from the Tree of Knowledge of Good and Evil, which leads us to all kinds of self-destruction and self-consuming evil acts. Some people are dismayed right now, thinking, *What is this man writing about?* and I get it. What is being inferred about the Tree of Knowledge of Good and Evil, and how does this tree relate to me? For starters, we will call it the Tree of Knowledge, and this abstract tree derives from an old biblical story, from the book of Genesis. However, this is not a promotion of the Bible and Western Christianity, or even religion for that matter. This is about experiencing limitless lives, and about extracting the most essential essence from one of the most famous stories from the Bible, the story of Adam and Eve. This story even predates the Torah. Even if you do not believe in the concept of God or gods, you will still be able to relate to the practical implications that are extrapolated from this story. My interpretation is inclusive and can be life-changing if you choose to peruse my text and my truth with an open mind and receptive heart. However, one must realize that there will always be a sliver of truth in all symbology or the retelling of one's truth.

With that being stated, my interpretation and this story's symbolic meaning should lead us into a deeper message that tends to lie dormant. As you read my words or other sentient beings' words, it is important to remember that adding words to a personal experience or feeling of truth will distort the authentic experience or truth. This is why I referenced that a sliver of truth will be found in all symbology because the absolute truth can only be experienced—never relived—with our descriptive words. Words (symbology) are employed to convey messages and to share our thoughts and experiences with other individuals; but this process requires an interpreter to have some baseline knowledge of our symbols or words to conceptualize and to decode our expressive messages. This is the rudimentary way to create and to share knowledge, and this is the birth of all societal lies and judgment—what is "right" and what is "wrong." These simple societal lies—such as national categories—end up being the most complex to detach from. Our national categories have become known as the knowledge of religions, races, ethnicities, genders, occupations, and sexual orientations; these adopted labels (lies) have conjured up inconspicuous and conspicuous judgments of what's "right" and who's "wrong" in our societies. We have witnessed the genocide of people. Many of us have also experienced rejections from this form of conditional love when our actions do not align with the expectations of others.

Hopefully, the above information enticed you all to want to explore my interpretation and my understanding of the story of Adam and Eve, and the nascent of our societal lies. The story of Adam and Eve purported that Adam was created from dust, and God (an infinite source of all life) breathed spirit into Adam, bringing Adam to life. God stated, "It is not good for man to be alone." This inspired

God to put Adam into a deep sleep and to remove a rib from him, and ultimately, to produce the infamous woman, Eve, as his helper. (Side note: this demonstrated the power of a woman, because man needed a woman to complete God's vision.) The message that I am attempting to convey is much deeper than a sexual connection or some connation to our sexual orientations—which is another label or lie created in our societies. Yet, the story implied that God told man he could eat fruit from any tree in the garden except from the Tree of Knowledge of Good and Evil; and if he disobeyed, he would surely die.

This statement is extremely powerful, metaphorically, and its context was never about a physical death. It was implying something much more sinister and much more permanent, in my humble opinion. I have heard this story told many times in churches and in schools, and most people tend to focus on what Adam was forbidden to consume in this story. This perspective is very similar to how many of us tend to view our modern lives. Most of us tend to focus on what we want in life and on what we do not have in life (to create an endless amount of suffering), rather than focusing on what we have in life (to produce an abundance of gratefulness and joy). However, I am getting ahead of myself. I will pivot back to this famous story (whether or not you agree with my subjective label of "famous," this story is considered well-known and revered in my world). Instead of focusing only on the thing that Adam was forbidden from having, we need to remember that he was given another choice in this story. Adam could have consumed fruit from the Tree of Life. This tree would have given Adam the wisdom, strength, power, and longevity of God.

This brings us back to the first sentence of this tome: Life is a mystery. Life can only be experienced, not explained by judgments of what is "right" or "wrong." Judgment is nested in our knowledge (i.e. Tree of Knowledge) or understanding of our finite human experiences. When we choose to make knowledge the foundation of our purpose, we end up consuming societal lies (e.g., "I am black and I am inferior to someone white," "I am a woman and I cannot lead like a man," "I am a homosexual and I am not worthy of love and acceptance," or, "I am dumb and I cannot learn math"). As the story reads, Eve was tricked into biting into fruit from the Tree of Knowledge because she wanted to become wise like God; and Adam easily followed her lead. I want us to pay attention to some details in this story. Initially, Adam and Eve were told to never even *touch* the fruit from the Tree of Knowledge because the touch sparks the thought, thought ignites action, action produces behavior, and behavior leads to a belief. We want to be like other people, so we bite fruit from their knowledge and reject self, causing us to wear masks and to hide our authentic form. Adam and Eve hid from God after consuming the forbidden fruit because they realized they were naked and ashamed to be around their maker.

Does this sound familiar? We hide from our age and cover our wrinkles with makeup and fancy skincare products, but more importantly, we hide from our self by being afraid to share our truths. Continuing the story, God said, "Who told you that you were naked?" This profound statement should challenge you throughout this book to ask, "Who told you that you are inferior to someone else because of the color of your skin?" "Who told you that you cannot be a leader because of your gender?" Who told you that you are unworthy of love and acceptance due to your sexual orientation?" and, "Who told you that you are dumb and not well-equipped to conquer manmade math?" These questions should lead you inward to develop some mindfulness questions and to "Check Your Life" (CYL): Be limitless. (Please note: CYL will be used for abbreviation purposes throughout the book, but remember, the power is in saying "Check Your Life.")

Chapter 4 will thoroughly discuss the multiple elements of

power contained in CYL This power can be used immediately by those who might be facing some brash of conflict, needing some drive to excellence, requiring love, and/or more importantly, aiming to unmask their true potential. In many of us, our authentic or true potential lies dormant and in wait, as the hero (us) awakens in our lives to capture it. Once we capture this mystical power and accept fruit from the Tree of Life, we will forever be changed; and we will start employing CYL to speak things into existence. Trust me, a better 'now' awaits—even if life is currently great—this book will challenge us to be even better, to be better than our best. We, as a society, need everyone to bring their best. We need heroes, and we need our full commitment to excellence. We are all uniquely made; if any of us doubt this declaration, I challenge you all to consider my following statement:

> *"There are roughly seven billion people on this planet. For us to be created, it required two individuals who met at a random time in our universe, to collectively create a 0.0000000003 percent chance to meet. Take into consideration that our parents would need to have some attraction to each other or some sexual encounter to produce an egg and 40 million to 1.2 billion sperm. Think about this, out of all of those millions of sperm, YOU were the sperms that made it through your mothers' eggs. Once again, this is less than a 0.000001 percent chance. We beat the odds to get here, so we are all created from a unique experience for some unique existence."*

Along this journey, this book will challenge you to question all learned knowledge and to question an authentic existence. I will admit as I wrote this book; it challenged me to ascend and to move beyond all preconditioned knowledge, so I could evolve into a limitless being. Please accompany me on this unpredictable journey, and

I will show you how to question life as you know it, and how to partake in the fruit from the most prosperous trees in our modern lives. We need each other to explore the truth, so we can shift to a new mind, a new spirit, and a new body, to produce a new energy that builds on one love for one world that lives for one God. This allows us to live a limitless life, with no mask, no labels, and no identities. We will be free—so "Check Your Life: Be Limitless" and journey with me to discover our authentic selves.

# Tree of Knowledge

*"Every human is an artist. The dream of your life is to make beautiful art."*

*-Don Miguel Ruiz*

The Tree of Knowledge appears to be a beautiful concept because our entire lives have been devoted to learning, exploring, gathering, and sharing knowledge. Our personal worlds—individual and societal—rely on information to build, to produce, and to accumulate wealth. In Western society, we are taught to consume products and services, to stimulate our wealthy society. A known spiritual and ancient proverb states, "People perish from their lack of knowledge." From my life experiences, all wise proverbs, ancient tales, and a majority of today's propaganda support the significance of acquiring knowledge. Even as a professor, I constantly encourage my students to seek more and to learn more; I pride myself on enhancing my knowledge by reading one book a week. The acquisition of knowledge serves as a boon in our society because our society uses knowledge to generate positional power. Knowledge should never be perceived as "bad" in common and uncommon conceptualization, even though I do not believe in a perceptual "good" or "bad." Knowledge becomes an extremely powerful ingredient when we choose to eat fruit from the Tree of Life instead of consuming fruit from the Tree of Knowledge. Both trees present images of juicy and delicious fruits. Yet, one tree serves a nutritious value, and one tree serves a deficient value. The Tree of Life serves prosperous fruit that injects nutrition to our exploration and to our extension of existence; the Tree of Knowledge serves poisonous fruit that judges and truncates one's journey and growth in life. The Tree of Knowledge of good and evil introduced our society to the notions of duality, opposites of attraction, and the concept of Ying and Yang.

This knowledge has destroyed the holistic beauty in our world and produced a concept of beginning and ending, as well as a mortal and immortal phenomenon to our existence. Most sentient beings no longer occupy a godly presence of limitless, and many of us have started pursuing our lives with finite, self-created limitations. When I refer to finite, self-created limitations, I am referring to finite human beings (us) who created labels of identity that include or exclude other finite beings from our tribes. Our decision to eat fruits from poisonous trees (such as the Tree of Knowledge) instead of fruits from prosperous trees (such as the Tree of Life) cuts ourselves off from limitless power and abundance. Every tree creates a pattern of flow, and each flow attempts to lead us on our pleasurable paths. One tree tends to focus on fleshly or hedonistic pleasures while the other tree tends to focus on spiritual pleasures.

The Tree of Knowledge flows as follow: learn + execute + believe = success. Yet, the Tree of Life abides by this design: believe + learn + execute = share authentic self.

When we enter this world, we enter as our authentic version, no mask or constructed labels. We have no conception of name, race, gender, citizenship, religion, and/or an understanding of comparison (e.g., what is beautiful or what is ugly?). These are all constructed labels that imprison our minds.

We run free, literally, naked of clothing and understanding of rules when we are born to this worlds. At conception, we are in the moment and allowed to be our authentic and unlimited selves until people teach us something different and make us feel the need to wear masks. I have come to learn that authenticity is the crux of any spiritual leader who lived limitlessly and who inspired the creation of a religion. Christianity's savior, Jesus, came to free people from their sins (e.g., anything that we do to harm ourselves or others) and remain in a god-state (i.e., freedom); Hinduism (the oldest religion) leads one to the ultimate release of worldly distractions (i.e., freedom); Taoism expresses a way to live in harmony with the Tao (i.e., freedom); Islam concentrates on a humble submission to God (i.e., freedom); Buddhism focuses on reaching a state of nirvana or enlightenment (i.e., freedom); Atheism maintains that nothing controls people and they can just be (i.e., freedom) by accepting life as is; and Shamanism reaches heightened states of consciousness, to interact with esoteric knowledge in the spirit world (i.e., freedom).

When I eat fruits from the Tree of Life, I view my thoughts with a beautiful sense of perfect understanding, void of labels. For example, a "tree" is viewed void of its label and seen as an erect object from the soil as some form of life, with no deep interpretation attached to it. Most religions operate under a sense of dogma and conditioned labels. I would argue that most religious individuals mean well and attempt to lovingly pursue life and interactions with others. The issue is that this manner of love tends to be distributed as conditional love—meaning we are loved and accepted if we adhere to certain rules. Personally, I have been both loved and rejected by overtly religious individuals. I have felt deep love and connection to these religious individuals as long as I followed rules within the religion. However, when I repudiate those rules, I have been ostracized, judged, and gossiped about by those same religious people. Many people have felt this rejection and know this rejection comes with confusion, shame, and guilt. All of those emotions are birthed through principles of knowledge, and knowledge of this form creates separation and division.

I want to clarify that this is not an attack on religion, because religion is a collection of practices to express and exercise one's spiritual beliefs. I surmise that, at the core, religion is a beautiful practice. Yet, religion tends to transform those individuals who focus on the imperialism of religion and who utilize religion to exclude and judge others into a powerful institution that suppresses the truth and destroys collective societies. Religions gain power when they can generate a massive or committed following. This collective idea, ultimately, makes people feel safe to practice their faith because there is strength in numbers. Also, people feel like their religion must be 'the true' religion if so many people are willing to follow—the assumption is that God cannot surely condemn us all to damnation. The truth is that religion constructs a combative duality or nature that opposes other religious sects of people who dare to practice a different set of beliefs. Numerous wars have been sparked by this exclusive perspective that lies hidden in most religious institutions. In most societies, the religion with the dominant voice and collective thought wins out and widens its sect of believers' collective ego, even though no finite being breathing has ever transitioned to the other side (e.g., life after death) void of our physical existence. When I refer to ego, I am considering Dr. Wayne Dyer's notion of E.G.O., to edge God out. Once again, religion can be something beautiful and can introduce us to everlasting spiritual concepts that tap us into esoteric realms and wonderful practical principles. However, religions have been the impetus of millions of deaths throughout our world, and the destruction was justified by religions and millions of their supporters who occupied similar beliefs. Where does this indoctrination of dogmatic religious principles and/or our beliefs originate?

Many of us probably have cogitated over this question before, and many of us know that domestication begins in our shared environments early on in life, when we are free to roam and express ourselves without the guise of rules and societal structure. I refer to this early domestication as the 'loud noise' phase of our lives, a period in time when many voices commandeer our minds. During this coup, we forget the true nature of our authentic selves, because we constantly gorge ourselves with fruit from the Tree of Knowledge. Periodically, I ponder over this question that was asked to Adam and Eve in the garden by their maker, "Who told you that you were naked?'" Every time that question enters my mind, I travel back in my mind to explore my domestication and my indoctrination process. I remember learning two seemingly opposing viewpoints: God is love and we should have no fear while embarking on the journey of life...but do not trust white people. At this time, I had no firm grasp on the differences of white and black, in regards to the construct of race. So, I was confused and bothered by this logic; something just never felt right in my being and spirit. This unsettling feeling prompted me to state, "If God is love and all-powerful, shouldn't I choose love instead of fear?" My statement created conflict because the two worlds met in a fearful state; my parents ate fruit from the Tree of Knowledge—and justifiably so, due to their personal experiences and classical conditioning. They believed in the taught construct of black and white in America, and they witnessed the atrocities experienced by their ancestors at the hands of white people. They had no desire for their kids to be the targets of systemic institution built on the power of one superior race (white) and one inferior race (black). However, I was still a pure child void of this knowledge and/or life experience, who had not yet eaten any fruit from the Tree of Life.

I believe most parents mean well and raise their children with good intentions to do them no harm. I also believe many parents teach their children unwittingly with their projected fears and illusions of what is best for their lives, even though they cannot hint at the depths of their children's souls and intentional consciousness. This knowledge of what is best for their children comes from an ignorance and axiom that a parent knows what is best for their child simply because they created and raised the child, not realizing that they're outward encounters. The real power happens internally, and no parent or loved one is privy to that knowledge. Most of us struggle to connect with our inner spirit as we venture through this physical experience of life. I strongly believe my parents meant me no harm and tried their best to protect me from the ills of our collective world. My parents experienced racism and mistreatment by the constructed race of white. However, the simple truth is that we still have a choice, regardless of the action (i.e., racism); we tend to create an instant reaction (e.g., something as a negative payback) instead of a proactive reaction (e.g., a well-thought-out response).

My statement was my choice of fruit, and it was judged or perceived as rebellion and disrespect because we were consuming fruit from opposing trees. My parents could not understand beyond their fear, so they did not understand my perspective. Their verbal and nonverbal disagreement was perceived by me as judgment because they were so far removed from a world void of labels. I was being introduced to classical conditioning and the dogma of race and religion in our segregated society. I had limited interactions with the knowledge of fear and the knowledge of race, enabling me to eat fruit from the Tree of Life. This allowed me to just be, believing that God was in the moments of not knowing. Let me clarify this statement again: not knowing certain information places me at peace with the present moment and causes me to accept that moment in its current existence. This shifts me into a state of spiritual knowing and worldly discernment of what is beneficial for my inherent nature. For example, I do not need to invest my time into knowing things I cannot control, if those things will make me feel negative and impede me from walking and acting in love. From my personal experiences, worldly knowledge (e.g., knowing information to benefit professional progression) requires human agreements to be understood while spiritual knowing becomes an intuitive personal experience that originates from the core of sentient beings.

I created a symbol that captures the essence of our choice to choose fruit from the Tree of Knowledge or the Tree of Life.

This image is a faceless or formless individual, with no race, no gender, no religion, no ethnicity, no political affiliation, no sexual orientation, and no known occupation. It is the authentic form of every sentient being, and its colors and symbology will guide us to the right fruits to choose and eat, as we progress through this physical experience called life. For example, white represents purity and peace, black is mysterious and beyond the comprehension of human form (esoteric), and red exemplifies passion, love, and/or strong desire. When we eat fruit from the Tree of Life (fruit to which I refer as the truth), we will always have a question mark in our minds. This question mark is an understanding that something unknown exists beyond our scope of comprehension by our finite minds. This question mark should remind us that it is impossible to state who we are or what we could be at our limitless level because there would be no label or no known knowledge to describe us. This image indicates that this formless individual has removed his or her mask and chosen to eat fruit from the Tree of Life. In this conscious-minded outlook, we can begin to walk around without our adopted masks, and we gain peace and freedom. Masks can be only embraced and viewed as successful by people who choose to consume fruit from the conditions found within the Tree of Knowledge. These masks are assigned roles, normally in the form of our vocations or relationships. When we eat fruit from the Tree of Life, we produce the power to separate ourselves from these roles and are able to remove those masks at any given time.

The right hand removing the mask represents power, authority, and guided blessings. The red background behind this individual indicates propulsion via love and passion, enabling "UnmaskYTP" to erupt from their core—known as the 'gut' by most people in my Southern upbringing. Those words stand for "Unmask Your True Potential," to live a life of authenticity, peace, and freedom. When we eat the fruit of truth, we live in a place of peace and abundance. However, it can be a state where we appear to be the only sober people within a drunken world. We will remove the scales and start to see our world with a fresh set of eyes, and we would stop competing with other sentient beings than ourselves. It will lead us on our own hero's journey, providing us with necessary sparks to discover the hidden treasure in everyday life with a heightened sense of interest. This journey will not stop tragedies or so-called 'bad' things (knowledge fruit) from happening in our lives, but it will give us the power to face those things with purpose, joy, and contentment. This new purpose-driven life will break our addiction to knowledge and mitigate the dangers associated with our assigned roles during our existence in our physical realms.

Before turning to the next chapter, we must take an introspective look deep within ourselves and ask ourselves these foundational questions:

- What tree of fruit do I consume on a daily basis?
- And, does this fruit enable me or disable me to live an authentic purpose?

# Assigned Roles

*"When you judge another, you do not define them, you define your-self."*
*- Dr. Wayne Dyer*

I know some of you are thinking, *What the hell is an assigned role?* I thought the same thing when this chapter was conjured up in my spirit and bounced around in my mind. Writing this chapter brought me back to some poignant memories from third grade, when my assigned seat was near a student who farted all the time and wiped his boogers on his desk. I apologize for this vivid memory, but it made me think about the assigned role I gave that kid. I told my friends this kid was disgusting, as I described his actions in detail to my clustered group of gossipers. These chosen gossipers shared my exaggerated story with others, and they taunted this kid and called him a loser. This kid was labeled immediately, and he was assigned several roles by me and other cruel kids: inferior, unimportant, nasty, helpless, stupid, smelly, and worthless. We were eating fruit from the Tree of Knowledge, and the saddest part is that he partook in the same fruit and accepted our lies—as gospel and/or the truth—not realizing his limitlessness resided on the inside. I would love to provide a happy ending to this story, but honestly, I do not know what happened to this kid. In my mind, I tell myself he beat the odds and went on to love others, in spite of our cruelty. Yet, the one thing I do know: if he continued to eat fruit from the Tree of Knowledge, he probably chose a common path and embarked on a path to placate others.

This memory and my thoughts about it come from a place of experience because I chose the common path for many years, trying to find validation in other peoples' opinions. I ate knowledge-enticing fruit for years, and my life was not a productive one, by my standards of success. For example, I was constantly suspended from school or in some form of in-school suspension. There were many days I wrote "James was here [date]" on in-school suspension desks, waited for my parents to pick me up due to school bus suspension, and entered school early for countless Saturday morning detentions. I was assigned the roles of thug, dummy, unworthy, ugly, hopeless, unimportant, funny-looking, and unwanted. My assigned roles made me happy to appear superior and to target an 'inferior' kid at that time, and this negative and self-designated attitude is the ultimate danger of eating the wrong kind of fruit and buying into societal lies. Who told us to accept these lies and why do we view these lies as significant? These two questions should inspire us to pick our fruit wisely. We need to take this sentence seriously because every decision is a decision to pick and engage in the appropriate fruit supply. Some fruit appears delicious and delectable, but too much consumption can fabricate a negative side effect within all of us.

For example, we are given assigned roles due to the systematic design of our society. These assigned roles are not inherently negative or dangerous, but our desire to accept any assigned role as our authentic self makes that given paradigm a lie to which we are masked. I am a son, brother, friend, parent, professor, actor, author, speaker, and leader, and these roles have been assigned to me by the people with whom I interact in my personal and professional life. All of these assigned roles allow me to serve as an effective actor in different realms during my physical existence; yet, a major problem occurs when I generate an imbalance in one assigned role, giving one more weight than the others. Naturally, I want to enjoy those individual roles without limitations and without adding more value to one, but something in my subconscious instructs me to focus more on work instead of being in the moment with my family and friends. On the contrary, while I am at work, my subconscious might motivate me to engage in lengthy conversations with my wife and friends. We are domesticated at young ages to accept fruits of knowledge and to reject fruits of life (i.e., being in the moment or neutral).

Domestication is a natural process for the human experience, even though this phase robs many of us of our innocence, truth, and unlimited potential. Parents, educators, religious leaders/seers, and family members teach us knowledge and share stories to provide us with a safe blueprint to survive and to live a fruitful life, without biting from the proper fruit. They notify us of our gender, race, color, religion, and family—which constrict our thinking and become instant limitations in our reactive state. I understand the unconscious pushback as you read about those stated assigned roles, and I agree that they are categories used to identify us in our collective societies. My aim is to encourage you to acknowledge those identifiers but to refrain from believing in them as your assigned identity. *Why?* you might ask. When we believe in those identifiers, we create complexity in our thinking. Yet, the truth should always be simple and transparent, never complex. Humans contrived those categories, and humans had to train us to agree with those categories—to make them acceptable, but not necessarily true. Remember, all humans are finite beings, with limited understanding and knowledge. Also, people's knowledge about other humans can never probe deep enough into their experiences to interpret their authentic being.

We are taught to interpret gender. Why? In most societies, it is to subconsciously impose acceptable rules and norms for males and females. This domestication has limited many women to think that they cannot compete with males in sports, mathematics, science, and/or any other male-dominated arenas. On the flipside, domestication has discouraged many men from becoming nurses, secretaries, school teachers, servers, and homemakers. Even as I type this text, I could sense my implicit biases swirling around in my mind, thinking to myself, *I would never be a homemaker*. I was domesticated at a young age to believe that a man takes care of the bills and should always find a way to provide for his wife and family. I personally believe homemakers have a tougher job, so I have embraced this assigned role, without attaching judgment to others who believe differently than me. Judgment is the main issue associated with accepting societal lies and with biting knowledge of assigned roles as a concrete concept.

When individuals choose fruits from the Tree of Knowledge, they have been indoctrinated to accept their way as being 'right' when compared to other peoples' perspectives. Most individuals gravitate towards other like-minded individuals who share a collective ego about knowledge, causing them to walk through life consciously and unconsciously evaluating people and situations. Life is now introduced in a form of duality or in measures of opposites. Most opposites are measured in superior or inferior positions. When I was assigned the role as a male, I was taught that it made me superior to a female. Yet, when I was assigned the role of being black, it was taught from an inferior comparison to white in U.S. society. My adolescent environment and my parents also assigned Christianity to be the dominant religion and the only way to God. The glaring issues with this knowledge were that I was taught to accept these rules and to refrain from asking questions to the adults (e.g., serpents from our modern gardens). However, Jesus, philosophers, thought-leaders, and seers were praised for their profound questions. Questions lead to exploration and to a neutral state of being engaged in the moment.

This neutral state existed prior to our domestication and to our collective indoctrination of cultures. We can all find this spiritual, godly, and neutral state when we venture into any inclusive childcare facility. Childcare facilities are filled with infants and toddlers of all genders, races, and colors, and who may or may not yet have been taught religions. These kids bite, wrestle, play, talk, hug, and kiss each other, with no thoughts of race, gender, color, and religion. These kids are driven by love, fun, and acceptance. They only eat fruit from the Tree of Life, loving in a manner similar to Jesus's life and other seers of significance spiritual influence, such as Buddha. During this phase of kids' lives, they display emotions, but they do not judge. Kids are taught to judge because adults no longer understand how to communicate through intuitive, nonverbal emotions. Kids see nothing wrong with defecating and pissing on themselves until they are taught to potty-train. We (adults) invade those child-like worlds of innocence and notify them that they needed to adopt and to conform to the behavior that we deem as right in our societies. Then, we become shocked as children speak their indoctrinated beliefs, calling their peers stupid, ugly, or some other offensive rhetoric.

A change in fruit and a shift in these kids' knowledge transmute their actions and attitudes from love to hate, from sharing life with classmates, to judging and bullying other classmates. When this paradigm shift happens, kids start to argue over being right or believing that they are more superior in thought, rather than arguing for the original aim of kids—to have fun and to explore. Once an individual becomes judgmental, indoctrination has this person seeking assigned roles and donning masks to placate the opinions of other people (e.g., parents' goals for one's life). My domestication commenced when my stepdad, whom I view as my father, adopted me and introduced me to Christianity. My family's influence was strong, and my parents' love was sincere and authentic. I believed my stepdad was the greatest man in the world, the closest man to perfection. I also believed that I had to accept Christianity or be doomed to a place where I would burn forever. I was terrified of this place, so I accepted the notion of being a certain way, in order to enter heaven when I died. In order to succeed in life, I thought I had to serve a religion and abide by rules. Yet, these rules and religion drove me further away from the Tree of Life and closeness to God and more towards the Tree of Knowledge and separation from my maker. Please do not take my statements as an attack on Christianity or any other religious doctrine, because I believe wholeheartedly in Jesus's life and its supporting principles, separate from the religion.

As you continue to the next chapter, I challenge you to ponder my previous thoughts and following questions.

- What religion did Jesus (or any other religious leader) belong to, prior to his demise?
- Did any religious leader have a deeper relationship with God (life) when compared to most of today's religious folk?
- If so, should we consider breaking away from our knowledge of religion and accept fruit from the Tree of Life and be neutral? When we continue to bite fruits of knowledge, we will wear masks and face the consequences that tend to follow.

# The Masking Process

*"Our lives begin to end the day we become silent about things that matter."*
~ *Dr. Martin Luther King Jr.*

There is nothing that lasts forever. Yet, the masking process materializes from a hidden belief that we need to protect ourselves from harm, or so-called 'bad' things. 'Bad' and 'good' are concepts enforced upon us during our domestication process, so we start to categorize things that please us or things that appease our gods (i.e., teachers or influencers) as good fruit. On the other hand, we reject and judge anything that oppose our checked boxes of good categories, provoking us to place conceptual labels of 'bad' on those opposing categories. We fear that if we do not operate within this safe zone of good, our influencers might consider us as bad—in our actions or overall physical form. Personally, I felt that any rejection meant I was unworthy of love and acceptance into heaven, this so-called final "resting place," reserved for saints in the afterlife. This mentality stymied me from having heaven on Earth and attracted me to many masks. I, like many of us, became the boy—and eventually the man—with many faces. I wore the mask of a Christian around my family and friends, due to the fear of dying and spending eternity in hell. Also, I wanted to make sure to see my Christian family and friends again in heaven, even though none of us truly know if we will recognize each other in the afterlife.

This mask led me to believe I could treat myself wrongly (sin) and enter a state of heaven when I die. My mask created my hell on Earth because I hated myself for never being good enough to attain perfection; I was always breaking man's rules (e.g., talking in class and not being a docile child in school). I wore a mask of being a black boy in a predominately white grade school, and this subjugated me to believe my intellect was inferior to my white classmates. I was told I would not be treated equally due to the color of my skin, and I bought that lie and sought any resemblance of that truth, even when many white teachers treated me with an abundance of love. If we seek, we shall find. I believed in negativity and donned that mask, and I was imbued with negativity. I know some of you are struggling to digest my previous sentences, and I would understand it if your thoughts rejected my unique truth. However, I want you to ask yourself some truly relevant questions. Who taught us that it is possible for people to hurt us if they treat us so-called unfairly? What does it look like to be treated fairly? If we are treated in a so-called fair manner, will it put other people in unfair situations? Would you care about the other people if you were treated fairly? Also, should we live in a world where there is no adversity? If so, why? As I cogitated over these questions, I asked myself, was it fair that I was born into a family that protected me from child predators or created me in a country that gave me an opportunity to pursue my self-interests? Or, is it fair that some people were born ignorant to our opportunities, but born to simple pleasures, such as holding a friend's hand or playing baseball with a stick and a bottle caps? Simple pleasures tend to be more appreciated in third-world countries, from my past experiences.

When my wife and I traveled to Havana, Cuba, I walked around with a sense of despair and tremendous sadness as I traversed their countryside. I made many mental judgments, and I thought it was sad that their citizens were not privy to my privileges. I assumed that many people were bored and unhappy due to their lack of electricity and internet access. I harbored these feelings as I continued to venture to different parts of Havana. It prompted me to converse with some of the natives, and instantly, my heart shifted from sadness for Havana to sadness for the U.S. These encounters allowed me to recognize another mask that remained hidden due to my knowledge of judgmental success. I constantly bloviated that happiness stemmed from gratefulness and contentment with the simple pleasures in life, but I was not living this powerful dream and/or wonderful state of heaven. Subconsciously, I thought joy derived from the acquisition of things, such as a comfy home and other wants (e.g., access to social media and other information that was not accessible in their country). I, like many of us, bought the lie that happiness is found in a quality car, home ownership, and a marriage and some kids.

I soon learned that all those external moments of happiness can also proffer moments of unhappiness and depression. When we wear this mask of success, we agree to the conditions of its forms of happiness. For example, most people are saturated with misery when they face financial hardship, divorce, or parenting difficulties. Yet, the crux of most masks is the plight for societal, familial, religious, and/or tribal validation. We are indoctrinated to desire acceptance from other people rather than acceptance from ourselves, inspiring external locus of control rather than an internal locus of control. The sad part is that we spend a majority of our life running from our authentic light to external noise, until a small percentage choose to seek their inner God and permanent joy.

This above statement is targeted at my brothers and sisters from my Western society, mainly in the U.S. We are taught at an incredibly young age to be the best, to compete with others, and to acquire external riches in order to possess some modicum of success. This paradigm has motivated many of us to abandon our authentic selves for some fictitious characters, becoming masked charlatans in this game of life. The essence of life is perennial and infinite, while knowledge is limited and finite. We tend to live our temporary lives in reverse, consuming manmade knowledge to lead us to an infinite understanding or experience—which never comes. This continuous and arduous pursuit causes us to mask ourselves to the edible lies (e.g., "I am a genius" or, "I am right"). A master of self understands that true knowledge leads one back to their inner self for life and luminous light and to an acknowledgement that it is not simply *what* we know, but *how* what we know sparks us to grow and to stay in the natural flow.

Flow is Christ, Chi, Dao, Love, Energy, and any other moniker for our conceptual understandings of God or supreme being. Natural flow is when we align our physical beings (i.e., avatars) with this deity or spirit, and ascend to a supernatural level. Our power happens and peace begins within this natural flow. This synergy and authentic voice produces a power that originates from the spiritual realm, but remnants of its power are always manifested in the physical realm. Many of us mask ourselves to this hidden power and operate from a limited range of power, serving our physical beings from an inferior position of thought. When we probe deeper into the masking process, we understand that this position of thought originates from the intellectual mind. All power dwells in this majestic place, where over 60,000 thoughts are generated each day within our finite minds. The conundrum is that most people will die and never tap into this limitless power that transcends our physical pain or any scarcity known in our finite minds. I am willing to guess that 95 percent of most people die guarding and believing the lies that were told to them by human serpents. The masking process is responsible for homicides, suicides, genocides, and any other divisions that separate humans from interacting with and loving each other.

We (humans) wear our masks so tightly that it blinds us from understanding true love, causing us to view other beings as objects that threaten our beliefs. These beliefs serve as the foundation for our many masks; all our adopted beliefs tend to drive us farther away from our inherent truth—a truth that is only privy to us, the individual experiencer. For example, I was told by my parents that I needed to speak and to act a certain way if I planned to succeed in U.S. society, because my parents were raised with similar adopted beliefs. Many black children were instructed to be more docile, because many of our parents lived with this fear and projected this fear onto us through their childrearing. When parents raise children out of fear, they end up impeding their authentic voices. I ate this fruit of knowledge for many years. And, my desire to consume these poisonous fruits limited my thoughts and my innate abilities. My inherent nature did not take kindly to capitulating to the fear of another being. This motivated me to buck this indoctrinated system to fear another being due to a constructed idea of color. I have learned that the truth is hidden in our inspiration to buck any form of dogma. I was determined to rebel and to act out because I was in search of the 'real me,' so to speak. However, my bucking against my parents' system constructed a pseudo "thug" version of myself that was not an authentic version of me, either. It was not until decades later and after a deep stripping away of myself that I unearthed my inherent truth and my profound understanding of life. I had to strip myself of self (e.g., all taught beliefs, ideals, and opinions of right and wrong) because my masks or lies were anchored and buried under these well-constructed truths. As long as we hold any human-produced beliefs, we will never uncover our truths and our authentic version of "self." This is the only way to begin eating the proper fruit; a healthy diet of life food for the living, rather than toxic food for the walking dead.

Both parties enjoy their respective food, but only the living food produces continuous joy within our authentic forms. Sometimes the living—or those who are seeking the fruit from the Tree of Life—indulge in poisonous foods from the Tree of Knowledge, and they end up getting sick or feeling convicted. For example, when I eat fruit from the Tree of Life, I understand that it is better to be slow to speak, be slow to get angry, and be quick to listen (James 1:19). This life-giving fruit creates peace and neutrality in my conversations, enabling me to accept these interactions as moments, rather than something (so-called) negative or (so-called) positive. Yet, my actions tended to differ at times when I conversed with my wife in past arguments. I would eat fruit from the Tree of Knowledge and think things like, "She is my wife (label), and I must help her." Subconsciously, these judgments made me perceive my wife as a victim, and inferred that she was incapable of assisting herself. I would use this information to decide that she was not worthy of my love at this juncture or during a given argument. My skewed and judgmental mindset triggered me to react in a negative manner, to be quick to speak with a louder tone, to be quick to get angry, and to be slow to listen. This, in turn, prompted me to disregard her feelings and her existence during our conversation, which served as the nexus for many of our arguments.

When I unmasked myself from labelling my wife, I also unmasked myself from the belief that my wife was my property. I do not own my wife, and she does not own me. We identify as a couple and play roles as husband and wife, but I no longer subjugate myself to the domestic beliefs of marriage. Most of us are taught advertently and inadvertently that we should control our spouses, as well as other individuals. The unmasking process will be discussed more thoroughly in a later chapter. I will explain how I confront uncomfortable conversations and eliminate judgment, anger, and inappropriate actions. But prior to discussing these strategies, I believe we should spark curiosity with extremely specific questions.

- Why do you fall into the trap of arguing with people?

- Where does this anger come from?

When we evaluate arguments objectively, we can easily diagnosis symptoms; we tend to struggle with identifying the root of the problem. But ultimately, the root of all problems tends to come from eating rotten fruit. Fruit that is averse to the inherent nature of a being and to an embracement of life should be viewed as rotten fruit because it is not prosperous to our authentic voice. A healthy decision can shift our thinking from a combative fruit and an argumentative mindset to a mindful fruit and a neutral mindset. This neutrality causes us to flow with life instead of building a resistance to life. There are many proven ways to position ourselves into a state of mindfulness, and I have tried many of them. However, the only thing that stuck and transformed my desires into positive actions was my personal powerful phrase. Check Your Life: Be Limitless.

# Check Your Life (CYL)

*"To think in terms of either pessimism or optimism oversimplifies the truth. The problem is to see reality as it is."*
~ Thich Nhat Hanh

Mindfulness has been mentioned earlier in this book, but what is it, really? Most of us view mindfulness as a catchy keyword, or a trendy buzzword without possessing sound understanding of how to implement mindfulness in practical ways throughout daily activities. So, what is mindfulness? And, why is it so important to our mental, physical, and spiritual evolution as beings? Contextually, mindfulness is one's ability to notice a thought, action, or intuition in the present moment, while refraining from attempting to interpret or challenge those present moments. In practical, everyday mental situations, practicing mindfulness gives me the ability to sit in a traffic jam without assigning judgment to that particular situation. The situation is simply viewed as a "just life" encounter. For example, I do not complain—subconsciously or consciously—about the given encounter; it is not even a conjured thought, enabling me to sit in a state of neutrality or calm. When I run for long distances, lift weights, cut grass, or wash dishes, I often find myself drifting into a state of mindfulness. Sometimes, I live in this state of consciousness throughout an entire day, but it is normal to fall in and out of states of consciousness. It is extremely difficult to be fully present for every second; however, I believe the more we strive for constant and consistent states of consciousness, the more we stay fully engaged in the present moment. I refer to my moments of consciousness as subtle shifts of impactful mindfulness.

There are many triggers during my physical experience that drive me into productive states of mindfulness. When I am challenged by physical pains, with a target of lifting a specific weight, or a challenging acting role. I use those moments to generate force and energy to just focus on given tasks until my mind only acknowledges the targeted task at hand, and nothing else—no distractions (limitations). When this phenomenon occurs, I refer to it as "locking in," prompting me to say, "I am locked in." This is my calm zone, and this is the only zone where I can meet some major obstacle head-on and easily conquer it. We must understand that to conquer does not mean to reach some worldly idea of success. To conquer means to learn, to improve, and to ascend to a higher level of personal success. This outlook should always drive us inward for internal validation rather than outward for external approval. This becomes a place of nonresistance, and it is in this place where friction and static dissipate. Most people are resistant to any change or situation that launches their emotions into a realm of uncomfortableness. We live to seek comfort, attempting to be Goldilocks in the popular fable, "Goldilocks and the Three Bears", who sought a life of ease. Yet, in order to evolve and to become limitless, we must find a way to become comfortable with uncomfortable or unknown situations, to dwell effectively and efficiently in circumstances of discomfort.

Acquiring power from situations of discomfort or potential discomfort, CYL aims to generate power within every second of every day. Every second presents an opportunity for discomfort or disease, and those precious seconds permeate potential poison throughout our day until we either avoid it or let it consume us. We need to acknowledge that disease is designed to create dis-ease in our lives because dis-ease constructs distractions; and distractions stymie our ability to manufacture inner power. Most situations contain some bad elements that conjure dis-ease. Yet, CYL gives us the power to see righteousness or signposts hidden in those uncomfortable situations, marking and lighting pathways to our individual heavens in this physical realm. Heaven resides within all of us, and all its prosperous roots dwell in our words—meaning we can speak wealth and health into fruition. I understand it may be difficult to believe in this idea of speaking health and wealth into existence because many of us envision health and wealth as tangible, things we can see and feel in the physical realm. We might also argue that I (or someone I know) am dealing with hypertension, diabetes, cancer, or some other physical ailment. First off, health and wealth dwell in our minds, and they can only be experienced in our physical realms when we capture them in our minds and believe beyond our visual beliefs. Dis-ease or diagnoses should be used to spark my mantra, "Check Your Life" because they are designed to shift us into a state of heightened awareness.

For example, I was diagnosed with hypertension in the summer of 2014. I drove to the emergency room (ER) because I had a severe headache and felt weak, unable to stand comfortably. The nurses performed some routine tests, as well as some typical medical procedures—measuring my height and weight, and checking my blood pressure vitals. The nurse immediately became alarmed by my blood pressure reading, so she took multiple readings over a 30-minute span of time, to be certain that reading was correct. My blood pressure was recorded as 210/195. The ER doctor informed me that my blood pressure readings placed me in dangerous company of a potential stroke or aneurism. He prescribed medication to reduce my blood pressure to a manageable and healthy level. The problem was that my prescribed medication impacted my blood flow, giving me weak erections and myriad dizzy spells throughout the day. Up to this point, I conditioned myself to believe that hypertension ran in my family and labeled hypertension as a hereditary condition, so I unconsciously ate fruit from the Tree of Knowledge. I was so full from those lies that I decided not to take another bite and calmly said, "Check Your Life." This placed me into a heightened state of consciousness and conjured a powerful moment in which I was grateful for hypertension, knowing that this experience would provide me with an opportunity to grow—mentally, physically, and spiritually.

Without my hypertension diagnosis, I would not have awoken to the seriousness of my poor health and improper nutrition intake. CYL functions as a natural concomitant with gratitude, making it a natural flow to our purpose-driven lives. This beautiful concoction constructed a dream state for me, a state where I had the most fit physique, with toned arms and sculpted abdominal muscles. It fueled my mind, and I believed CYL supplied me with the confidence needed to change my diet (e.g., removing bread, sugar, and red meat) and to engage in strenuous workouts (e.g., five-mile runs and strength training). I started my health journey with joy and an unhealthy weight of 204 pounds. Yet, seven months later, I dropped to a healthy weight of 164 pounds, with toned arms and sculpted abdominal muscles that I had seen in my previous dream state. However, the more astonishing feat was that I no longer needed to take my hypertension medication and have not taken any hypertension medication in the last four years. My blood pressure has remained at a healthy level, and I am still pill-free.

Some people consider this a blessing or some form of power from God, not realizing this power lies deep within all of us. The true magic is in the belief, the magic is in CYL, and the power is the combination of belief and CYL. Jesus even stated, "Very truly I tell you, whoever believes in me will do the works I have been doing, and they will do even greater things"[2]. The lord proclaimed, "If you are grateful, I will surely increase you"[3]. Lao-tzu says, "Fortune owes its existence to misfortune, and misfortune is hidden in fortune"[4].

I developed power from gratitude for my situations—whether so-called 'bad' or not—and then I spoke with veracity that caused my belief to be greater than my unbelief.

- What challenges in your life enable you to believe beyond belief?
- What powerful phrases do you say to yourself to make you believe?

# The Power Behind CYL

*"Man is a universe within himself."*
~ Bob Marley

As a child, I believed in the lure of magic. Most children are drawn to the idea of magic, and many fables and children's books had a way of challenging me to dream and to believe in this idea of magic. Subconsciously, I was inundated with this notion to dream, and to dream big. Even as I grew older and began to enter a world that taught me to believe in labels and to inadvertently accept the thought of limitations, I held onto a small hope and belief in magic. As a youth, I was influenced by David Copperfield's (a popular magician of the '90s) ability to saw a woman in half and his countless card tricks that left me flabbergasted and inspired to become an amateur magician. When I was not watching David Copperfield, I perused television channels for other magicians who put me and so many others under the spell, "abracadabra." This spell is interpreted as, "As I speak, I create." I had no clue of that latent message in the '90s, yet I did feel an unspoken and unknown power when I heard those words uttered. I was transfixed by the verbal and nonverbal cues of the rhythmic saying. The power was in the belief and in the clandestine incantation, "abracadabra." Most people who heard this incantation believed or had a strong desire to believe, creating a vibrational power during this magical experience.

The phrase was merely chanted prior to the magician executing their supernatural trick or illusionary enchanting acts. People would be lulled into believing the magician every time the incantation "abracadabra" was uttered, while the magician spoke other words to follow this hypnotizing rhetoric. Those succeeding words were usually words that stated the magician's reason for casting their spell. Some sages surmised that the incantation 'abracadabra' was so powerful that it was spoken in some cultures to cure physical illnesses, but I would argue that our greatest illness as people is the loud chatter and constant destructive talk between our ears. This illness becomes cancerous and metastasizes in our minds, spreading its poison from our minds, to our hearts, to our actions, and ultimately to form our habits. That formidable illness has stopped more people from living their authentic inner voice or God-inspired lives than any other physical diagnosis. It leaves us walking around as unconscious zombies, engaging in pointless conversations and interactions. This unconscious condition of existence frightens me more than ruminating about my final seconds when I will fight to gasp for my last breath or my body stiffens, to move no more in this physical realm.

CYL is spoken to ensure that I live every single second of every single day as if it might be my last moment having a personal experience on this earth. Death is inevitable and no one is immune to this beautiful conclusion to our physical understanding of life. CYL attractive magic (power) is merely activated by a litany of routines that commence as soon as I awaken to my morning consciousness state. When I sleep at night, my prefrontal cortex becomes dead to our conscious worlds. My subconscious is manipulated sometimes prior to drifting off into my dreamland state, using a routine I coined as **priming the pump**, an action taken during a recessionary period to boost the economy. However, **priming the pump** means to boost my subconscious brain as my brain wanders off into my unique dreamland. I carry out this action by using headphones to listen to some guided mediation or positive affirmations. This is an attempt to develop a subconscious program susceptible to positive words that evoke magical power, better known as the law of attraction. This contrived a paradigm shift and devised a new subconscious program that produced a robust faith in magic.

Christianity is the dominant religion in the Western world, but many Christians do not believe in magic, from my personal experiences. Many religious zealots are quick to label (e.g., eating fruit from the Tree of Knowledge) magic as demonic or some unique form of witchcraft. Personally, I know some parents who considered the *Harry Potter* book series as demonic because it did not support the dogma of Christianity, in their opinion. Many separate magic from both religion and science, placing it on an island with witches and/or sorcerers. The glaring difference, to me, is that magic does not operate under the rules of empirical science or organized religion; both science and religion function under limitations, while magic is boundless without limitations to produce limitless power. This reminds me of the most popular limitless figure in Christianity, Jesus, who dwelled all power from the spirit, Christ. Christ spoke and God (e.g., an omnipresent and ubiquitous spirit that adopted the conceptual name of God) empowered him with the power to heal and to bless people. Christ conspicuously broke religious rules set by priests and other seers of his time, making him limitless and free of manmade rules and set limitations.

A woman was caught up in the act of adultery (having relations with a married man), so she was brought before Christ for judgment; but Christ stated, "He who is without sin cast the first stone"[5], now, "Get up and sin (e.g., anything to harm one's self) no more"[6]. Religious zealots followed laws that insisted that women should be stoned to death for committing adultery. There is biblical text that supports the stoning of women, yet not of men...but that is another story for another book. Power has the ability to influence the course of events by invoking supernatural forces in our earthly events. We should reflect on our lives and dig deep into our past and try to discover moments when magic was injected in our earthly events. As I dive into my past, I am reminded about a time when I almost drowned. We were celebrating a family gathering at Gaston Lake in North Carolina. I was about five years into my marriage, so I was 24 years old and a fit athlete. I was chatting with some of my wife's cousins on a pier when our conversation shifted towards my ability to swim. I said, "I am a strong swimmer, and I can swim from the pier to shore." Her cousins dared me, and I took the bet. One of her cousins asked me if I needed a life jacket, and I responded, "no, I am good."

I jumped in and doubt instantly crept into my mind; but I began to swim furiously. About halfway to shore, I felt a burning pain and noticed my desire slowly fade out of my body. I started doggy paddling to stay afloat, but this action made me extremely lethargic. I cast aside my fatigue and commenced to swim harder and faster. About 20 feet from shore I yelled out, "I do not think I am going to make it!" I dipped under the surface of the water, and I panicked, kicking and paddling even harder. As my inner dialogue became dire, I start thinking, *I cannot believe this is how I would die...what will people think about me dying by drowning?* When I got about 10 feet from shore, I attempted to stand up, but there was no sand under my feet, and my head went underwater. I fought to stay afloat, and I kept kicking. I yelled out one more time, "I will not make it!" and my wife's cousin said, "You can stand up here." I put my feet down, and they landed on a solid foundation. I collapsed as soon as I was safely on shore. When I revisit this story, I see the supernatural forces breathing, to make it my survival story. Every situation in our lives has some element of supernatural forces. It is our job to analyze our lives and to find those daily spiritual victories. If we did not go out of our way to attempt to humanize this supernatural energy or ubiquitous spirit labeled "God," we would not have a hidden fear of the words, supernatural, energy, law of attraction, or power. We tend to fear the unknown and things that we cannot understand, so we go out of our way to label everything, to dispel those fears. However, it does not stop at this manmade use of terms because we have countries and people who will commit murder in the name of their religion or way of expressing their ubiquitous and omnipresent God.

Once again, we fear the unknown; in religion, we fear what is different from our beliefs because religion is tied to our transition to the afterlife. If this seems confusing to you, you are not alone. I was confused until I understood the seductive power (magic) to follow the collective ego (e.g., dominant opinion in society) that permeated our society and my personal world. Our collective ego tends to cast a collective thought which, in turn, casts a magical spell on its members—us. For example, there was a point in time when identifiable white (e.g., constructed belief of a collective group to refer to superiority at the time of invention) Christians devised a collective thought that enchanted other Christians to buy Africans as chattel slavery during the Atlantic slave trade. I viewed this as deceptive magic that impacted the course of events for Africans and America for over 400 years, and it significantly influenced the remaining remnants of racism and prejudice ideologies in America. To me, Christ was the first magician to influence my limitless life because Christ was limitless, without a religion or a set of manmade rules. [Note: I am not referring to Christ as a magician to demean or to disrespect, I am stating to demonstrate his power and its relation to our untapped power.] In my opinion, we are Christ and Christ is us. When a sick woman sought healing by reaching out to touch the hem of Christ's garment, he replied, "Your faith has healed you"[7]. I viewed this interaction as a magical moment that required belief (e.g., she surmised a touch could heal her), words (e.g., spoken with veracity), and action (e.g., the woman's effort).

Christ informed the woman that her power laid internally instead of externally. From my experiences and interactions, religious individuals rely on an external power to intervene in their daily affairs, rather than believing and knowing as the sick woman who reached out to Christ. Many people believe in universal laws, such as the law of attraction I previously mentioned. My interpretation is that the law of attraction implies that our desires and our beliefs must be on the same frequency prior to attracting something stated or envisioned in one's mind. I can argue that this is a form of power because it simultaneously raises the frequencies of both our desires and our beliefs, to manipulate a course of events. Personally, this shifts my mindset from negative to positive, and it will happen for you as well, but only if you believe in manifested power. CYL powerful underpinnings are tethered by a robust belief and an unremitting desire for something, but it is only activated by my conscious words and a tangible vision of me living that latent desire. The only caveat to consistently producing power in our lives is that we must walk in our authentic spirits and not wear adopted masks. For example, there were times when I wore the mask of being a thug—a negative force. However, I tapped into my authentic spirit and used my athletic football ability, producing power during football games where I ran for over 200 yards and scored multiple touchdowns, even attracting the attention of college football scouts—a positive force.

Yet, when I attempted to earn a college scholarship, the universe did not enable me to attract a scholarship due to the overwhelming negative forces I created in my physical experience. My negative forces consisted of running away from home, dropping out of school, failing to study and to complete course assignments, selling drugs, fighting, getting suspended from school, and disrespecting people with negative words and actions, to name a few. Mathematically, my negative integers outnumbered any positive integers I generated in my life, creating a negative, disruptive, and destructive charge in my internal being. Ultimately, it served as the match to my thug life gasoline that laid dormant behind my mask of temporal change, a change that was employed to receive a scholarship from the universe. CYL challenged me to make drastic changes, and those conscious changes positively altered my universe forever. I birthed a belief that I could do anything as long as it was tethered to my authentic inner God and enabled me to manifest things in my individual universe, as a God.

I would not be shocked if the last three words of that previous sentence stirred up some confusion within some peoples' minds and spirits, because most people in my culture (Western society) were taught that there is only one supreme God. Religion-constructed tenets that limit our beliefs in this arena ultimately limit our power to produce magic and to become limitless. My position is not to convince you to adopt my beliefs; my job is to persuade you to explore deeply within yourselves and to awaken the infinite intelligence or God inside you. I will embed the following scriptures for my Christian readers, to spark you to think for yourself and to question any knowledge transferred to you from other finite beings (i.e., a pastor or fellow Christian). "And the Lord God said, 'The man has now become like one of us, knowing good and evil. He must not be allowed to reach out his hand and take also from the tree of life and eat, and live forever'"[8].

There are so many things to unpack from this thought-provoking scripture, but the most obvious is who the Lord God was conversing with when he said, 'be like one of us.' This scripture also explained the limited power and danger in eating fruit from the Tree of Knowledge because knowledge of good and evil raised our awareness to judgment, bringing subjective power to things, situations, or people considered superior. This scriptural text also highlights the power of consuming fruit from the Tree of Life which proffers up an unlimited power to live free. I interpret the notion to live forever as the power to live free, and to me, that is the true power behind CYL. It supplies us with the power to face ALL our fears (e.g., lies we were told packaged as our beliefs), and the power to face our greatest fear—self. Yet, we must probe deep into our past and/or origin to address the big "why" or root to our fears.

- What labels do you feel limit you?
- How can you utilize CYL to discover your power?
- What are some situations in your life where you recognized a supernatural intervention?

# Face ALL Your Fears

*"To hell with circumstances; I create opportunities."*
*~ Bruce Lee*

Fear is an inevitable element in our lives. Fear seems inescapable because it permeates our society and haunts many lives. Fear tends to be assigned a negative connotation. It consumes our mental and physical liberties, stopping us from tapping into CYL or our limitless potential, and eliminating our latent power. Fear and/or any label is something that generates an unpleasant emotion based on a belief that something is potentially dangerous or threatening. However, we need to pay attention to the fact that it is a *potential* threat, not necessarily a threat to our being. When we capitulate to these potential threats, it stops us from progressing towards our individual excellence in our individual (personal) worlds. Why should we allow any potential threat to captivate us with fear? Fear can raise our level of awareness to some form of psychological or physical threat, or even to a deeper understanding of "why" we are engaging in this fearful event. Yet, the so-called fearful event is only as scary as we conceptualize it in our minds, no matter the threat. Some people show no fear, even in the face of imminent death, because they have envisioned death as a natural process. Some people even believe death is better than this temporal living.

For example, Thich Quang Duc, a Buddhist monk, chose self-immolation (e.g., burning himself to death in a meditative, seated position) to protest for religious equality on June 11, 1963. Duc's "why" was greater than enabling his spirit to dwell longer in his physical avatar. When our "why" supersedes fear, there is no element on this planet that can stop us from living freely and sharing our limitless power. The funny thing is that the answer to our "why" is irrelevant; I contest, from my experiences, that the feeling that we are acting on behalf of something greater drives us to meet and to embrace fear. On the contrary, we will quietly seek out or welcome fear into our lives because we know that the greatest gifts or pleasures are on the other side of fear—making fear a "must." I absolutely adore situations or encounters that challenge me or generate a measure of anxiety in me, because they require me to amplify my degree of focus to generate limitless power. My power derives from my finding comfort in uncomfortable circumstances.

I speak my positive affirmation and perform my power-inducing routines to produce limitless power. My conscious routines are presented at the end of this section, and I surmise that anyone can immediately implement my routines for powerful impact, and in any conflicting situation. I will preface the previous declaration with this spell-breaking statement:

**Everything you see is an illusion of tangible and intangible objects that we choose to assign reality and psychological-induced meanings to.**

**Power-Inducing Morning Routine**

1. **When I become conscious (awake) in the morning, I state—either with my eyes opened or closed—that today could be my last day on this earth. (I believe this with all my heart, which makes it real and inspires me to move and to make the most of my day.)**
2. **I smile and move to the edge of the bed and open my arms**

wide. Then, I take in three deep breaths (3-4 seconds inhale and 3-4 seconds exhale).

3. I find three simple things to be grateful for in my life. I always make these things personal to my being. For example, I might say, "I am grateful for my ability to see, breathe, and walk." However, I would not say, "I am grateful for my kids," because they are not my kids and they are external to my natural being.

4. I walk into the bathroom and smile at myself in the mirror, read my goals that I keep on a note taped to the mirror, and then I tell myself how amazing I am, in very descriptive words. For example, "James, you bring joy to the world, you are here to serve and lead, and you are a god." Then, I conclude this brief interaction with a smile of acceptance.

5. Next, I state my daily affirmation of love and life by speaking with power: "*Today is a glorious day, and for 86,400 seconds I will give my excellence and my best until I am laid to rest. I am abundantly blessed and never stressed...Check Your Life: Be Limitless.*"

6. I feed my spirit with some biblical scriptures, Buddhist and principles, African proverbs, and/or Creflo Dollar, Joyce Meyer, or T. D. Jakes sermons, as well as some inspirational videos. The point is that I feed my spirit with anything that evokes love and righteousness in my spirit.

7. Finally, I read and train, to educate my mind and to build my body; I do this in the gym or in my home gym. I lift and drift—I execute a superset of continuous strength training, and then read a couple pages of a book between sets.

Note: I also make my bed each morning when I am the last one to exit the bed. Making the bed is vital to starting our day

**off on the right track, because this simple feat provides us with a small win at the start to our day.**

My daily positive affirmations construct a power that provides me with the ability to face unexpected obstacles head on. I view my routines as a proactive measure to combat fear or anxiety-ridden circumstances. Fear is inevitable, as stated previously, and I strongly believe every individual will encounter something, some individual, or some situation that will produce a state of fear. Routines are implemented and practiced to mitigate and eliminate potential fear. My routines taught me to boldly seek out situations that might generate a level of fear in my flesh, acknowledging that any growth came when I faced some level of fear. Fear perched me in uncomfortable situations and those uncomfortable positions led me to seek solutions that manufactured solace in my spirit. Notice that I fastidiously stated "a level of fear in my flesh" because fear does not impact my spirit, and it never will.

Fear cannot negatively impact our spirits, if we eat fruit from the Tree of Life. This fruit does not label fear as something harmful; on the contrary, fear is perceived as something that heightens our level of awareness and puts us into a mindful condition. There are two fears that stymied my progression in life and limited my experiences in life. Those two fears were: a fear of dogs and a fear of heights. Both fears produced paralyzing trepidation at times in my being, and for decades I remained domesticated to these illusions of peril. However, when I began to live for something much greater than self, I challenged my limited beliefs of immediate harm. I said, "Check Your Life: Be limitless and face all your fears." I decided to repudiate the lies of limitations that served as a concomitant to my fears. I also noted that all my fears were anchored in my beliefs and experiences from my youth, and I realized that those beliefs did not exist prior to my spirit's encounter with other finite beings who consumed lies within this physical realm. Remember, all lies limit us and all truths expand and complete us.

As Jesus and many other sages stated, only the truth can set us free. I interpret that liberation as a free detachment from ourselves (egos) and societal lies, which tend to create mental hells; but on the contrary, our liberation produces heaven on Earth. An abundant life awaits all of us when we employ a valiant effort to confront all self-created and world-associated lies.

Let's revisit my fear of dogs and my fear of heights. Somewhere along my journey, I constructed these all-consuming fears and started to fill myself with the lie that all dogs bite and/or I will die if I position myself at precipitous heights. I trained myself to view dogs in the same manner that I viewed people, by making the conscious decision to stop eating fruit filled with the learned lie that all dogs will bite me. When we eat fruit from the Tree of Life, we realize our job is to experience life instead of labeling it with our illusions of fear. I conquered my fear of dogs and heights because both were transmuted to some kind of tangible fear, set out to harm me. This was true even when I saw owners enjoying the company of their dogs. I labelled other sentient beings as crazy when they scaled mountains or traversed to high heights. Mental maturity taught me that my experiences are born out of my interpretation and judgment of a condition. If I believe dogs will bite, my mind will stay transfixed on the notion that dogs intend to bite me. The same is true of heights. If I surmise all tall buildings are dangerous, I will be incapable of standing on top of the rooftop of a tall building. Both explanations come from authentic experiences. This realization has led me to limitless joys that I never thought existed. "For I know the plans I have for you declares the Lord, plans to prosper you and not to harm you, plans to give you hope and a future"[9].

- What are three of your biggest fears?
- How will you strategically face them?
- What are the positive outcomes if you choose to face them?
- What are the limitless possibilities if you conquer those fears?
-

# Joy is on the Opposite Side of Fear

*"He who has overcome his fears will truly be free."*
*~ Aristotle*

As I child, I learned to chase happiness, not yet realizing that happiness is a temporal state. The Declaration of Independence even discussed the importance of American citizens' pursuit of happiness; the land of the free touted this importance in one of its most significant documents. Happiness is a state of being happy, which means we find pleasure in some endeavor, thing, and/or person for a span of time. However, joy raises the bar to a great state of pleasure that transcends happiness. The sad thing is that many people die without ever experiencing a relationship with joy because many people seek out temporal happiness or pleasures in external things. It was normal for me to witness people complain about work all week until Friday. On Friday, all of those complaints suddenly would transform into boasts about the weekend's plans: getting blackout drunk, hooking up and having one-night stands, and frivolously spending money on some weekend social event. On many days and weekends, I sought similar temporal happiness. I stayed in this complacent state because I was afraid to be seen as weak or different within my unique environment.

In my environment, peers who did not attempt to conform to the in-crowd or influencers were teased and/or bullied. I faltered in this environment, and I hid behind consistent and constant fear. I battled two types of fears: physical and psychological trepidation. I also suffered from the 'small man complex,' feeling that I had to be even tougher in an environment that incited violence. The subconscious mentally seemed to be 'only the strong survive.' The conundrum was that my suffocating milieu made me believe that my illusion to fit in and to be 'normal' was my reality and accompanied self-sustaining joy. Our fears have a way of conjuring feelings that can impact us from the depths of our stomachs to mind-altering needs to escape, physically and mentally, not realizing that joy comes after we face our fears. My first life-altering fear started prior to my conspicuous fears of dogs and heights. This glaring fear was the divorce of my biological father (Richard).

I will preface this discussion with a positive disclaimer: I was blessed with an amazing dad (Jimmy) whom I accepted as my original earthly father. These two examples provided me with a splendid example of a label and a belief. There are subtle and overt messages that place bloodline or family members above individuals who do not share the same bloodline. This is the first form of a tribal mentality—a mentality that encourages us to gravitate towards people who are perceived to be like us. As a child, I ate fruit from the Tree of Knowledge and accepted the lie that blood relatives trump non-bloodline friends, making me devalue Jimmy, an individual who loved me unconditionally as a child. When I finally ate fruit from the Tree of Life and experienced the unconditional love of Jimmy, I forgave Richard and let that lie (bloodline) go and accepted Jimmy's love as authentic and transcending bloodline. This gave me a joy beyond any comparison, and it helped me overcome the fear of needing validation from Richard, while loving Jimmy unconditionally.

Remember, joy is unspoken freedom. Many people view joy as this constant state of peace and contentment. This is something I do not disagree with at all. However, this sustained peace and contentment arrives when we liberate ourselves from the domesticated lies and societal norms of being a specific way, outside of our authentic selves. I was afraid to let go of my biological father's ghost and to love Jimmy in the present because I was taught the adage, "blood is thicker than water," a reference to blood ties being stronger than nonblood ties. When I finally let go and loved, love became the catalyst to conquering fear and sustaining joy. Labels or knowledge stopped me from unconditionally loving Jimmy, but as I flowed with the experiences of life; those restrictions that were tied to labels, fell off and brought me to my truth. Fear does not merely hide in labels. Fear shows up in the midst of love. The most common love is in romantic partnerships, serving as a rival to vulnerability. Many people enter romantic partnerships with love in their hearts and a protective wall to buffer a potential heartbreak.

My marriage vacillated between potential greatness and potential disaster, and I played a significant role in this crazy pendulum between being in love and out of love. I was afraid to open up completely and to be vulnerable because I was afraid of giving all of myself and losing my shield to possible heartbreak in the process. I wanted to play it safe by limiting my commitment or collective investment, not knowing that this decision was the impetus to my limited joy. Joy was waiting for me on the opposite side of my fear, but I was too afraid to risk heartache in the process. The gamble seemed too grand from my finite conditional love, especially when I was able to bask in temporal moments of happiness. Limited happiness sufficed during 18 years of marriage, even though I knew this was the woman God gave to me. Yet, as I continued to evolve in mind, body, and spirit, my limitless soul yearned for and dared for more. My soul wanted to immerse its limitless potential within limitless joy, to explore all the hidden power within unconditional love. I finally found this joy when I probed deeper within myself and destroyed the remaining identity of James and his idea of safety.

When I took this introspective dive, I admitted to myself that James and safety were illusions of my mind produced to protect me (e.g., my designed identity). Once those masks were discarded, I stopped consuming those delicious lies that I had to be right, that I had to be heard, that I had to be validated by my wife's love, and that I had to be in control of our relationship (note: the powerful word "our" makes this a partnership rather than "my" singular relationship). These were some of the glaring challenges I had to overcome to experience joy. Even though I knew my wife was the greatest blessing I received during my existence, I was too afraid to fully invest and to face my challenges. The thought of fully investing in our relationship frightened me to the core because I did not have the mental fortitude to be vulnerable. I had to search deep for some power to free me from this fear because my fear hid my truth—and my truth was the key to open the locked door of freedom.

> *"Check Your Life: Be Limitless...I validate me, I love me, and I will face my fear and be vulnerable. I will continue to live this way, even if I lose the most amazing woman in my life, even if I lose my physical life in the process. I will be free and stay free."*

This declaration proffered me the inspiration and passion needed to share my deepest pains, insecurities, and shortcomings with my wife. I accepted the truth that everything ends, so I needed to capture every moment, in every second I have experienced thus far and will experience in the future.

I acknowledged that playing it safe did not create permanent solace and joy. On the contrary, it created constant bickering and frustration that I could not seem to quell. I became a slave to my selfish thoughts and hidden desires. My intuitive spirit and visceral instincts knew that solace and joy came from within. I wanted to believe it was safe to hide my fears behind a tough exterior, which presented an all-powerful display to others and an attitude of having it all together. But I did not realize that this mindset placed me on an isolated island, with no connectivity to other sentient beings.

We were contrived to have interdependent partnerships to survive and thrive. We were placed in this physical realm to produce successful relationships. Yet, partnerships can create a slippery slope of codependency, which is an extreme form of relying on a partner to survive. My personal relationship with my wife shifted from codependency in the inaugural years of our marriage, to independency and to conditional love. Eventually, my declaration to myself led me to check my life and to be independent and to be committed to an interdependent partnership without conditions.

I would no longer play it safe. I had to venture into my realm of fear and see what awaited me on the opposite side. Personal relationships tend to present our greatest challenges with fear because we deceive and lie to hide our true natures. We do this in fear of offending or losing the interest of our lover. Interestingly, I found a deep inner joy and connection to my wife that I had not thought existed. Up to that point, I thought I had to place controlling conditions on my relationship in order to produce some joy and some peace in my marriage. The joy and solace came in my relationship with my wife when I decided to relinquish control and started to love without conditions. Fear can be debilitating, but motivating at the same time, to construct an oxymoron philosophically. Charles Swindoll said, "Life is 10% of what happens to us and 90% of how we respond to it." When fear is perceived, it creates temporary stress, giving us an opportunity to use it as either motivation or hindrance. Stress has a negative connotation, but researchers have proven that there are two types of stresses: good stress and bad stress. Good stress serves as an impetus to inspire us to move or to survive during a physical threat, and to act or to make changes during a perceived threat (not actual). Bad stress causes us to stop moving during a physical threat or to complain and/or blame during a perceived threat which leads to anxiety (chronic stress).

Why is this scientific lesson about stress important at this juncture in this book? To me, it is another example of the power of labels. Many of us perceive fear and stress as something negative because society's collective ego suggests that those terms are negative and detrimental to individual progression. We eat those lies and never question the authors of those lies, consuming label (e.g., all stress is bad) after label (e.g., weak people embody fear). We must be willing to face the truth and understand that fear hides behind labels, trusting that the truth will free us from our overt and subtle fears. Fear of self is the greatest enemy because we are afraid of addressing our faulty software programs (e.g., believing you are going to hell if you question God). Our belief and thought systems derive from installed software programs from our unique environments. When I uninstalled my old software programs and questioned my authentic nature, I produced customized software that was DNA-specific and this created a new paradigm. I realized I am a god, and I am limitless. We all are gods and/or sentient beings who are capable of being limitless and who have the ability to make our vessels capitulate to our celestial DNA. Read the following paragraph again and again until you truly believe what I wrote, because I found joy on the opposite side of all fears when I truly believed I was a god and limitless beyond any human measure.

- What are some of your greatest fears? Choose one fear and face it today, right now.
- What did you learn when you faced your fear? If you are still alive, I am sure that you are energized to attack life.
- What is your major takeaway from facing this fear?

# *Courage and Creativity: Attack Life and Be in the Flow of Now*

*"He who is not courageous enough to take risks will accomplish nothing in life."*
*~ Muhammad Ali*

The universe, infinite intelligence, or God spews excellence in every atom, and I would argue that every atom has a specific purpose. I would also argue that every atom originates from a more perfect creator, and human beings are the greatest of all finite creations known to mankind. I surmise that something infinite and with a higher consciousness birthed the atoms permeating throughout the human body. If this something (i.e., God or infinite intelligence) is greater, we are greater and more limitless than we ever could have imagined. We have been limited at birth due to our strong desire to label everything. We have a propensity to want to know the name, origin, etc. of every person, place, or thing we encounter. Our need to know derives from a place of fear, and this place inserts limitations into our way of thinking, reacting, and living.

Fear should be viewed as a necessity for courage and creativity. Our greatest innovations and discoveries were birthed from some element of fear or objectivity of the unknown. I know your minds might be going crazy at this moment because fear is constantly assigned a negative connotation, causing many of us to view fear as this monstrous event or immovable obstacle. Fear is anything that raises our anxiety about an unknown circumstance. In addition, fear is a natural occurrence in our lives, and is significant to our survival in some situations. Fear assisted our ancestors or primitive brothers and sisters to survive the dark and dangerous beasts lurking in all corners of our vast planet during the caveman era. Let's revisit the two types of fears again: physical and psychological. These fears should be understood as both external and internal power, which I understood to mean good stress (external) and bad stress (internal).

These fears are absorbed and transformed into good stress or bad stress, but only good stress can be transmuted into an internal motivator. The easiest way to comprehend this is to remember that good stress does not impede our internal well-being; instead, it presents a challenge—better yet, an opportunity for internal growth. Bad stress destroys and plants internal land mines, causing us to self-implode in the long-term due to the internal damage of this form of stress. An old African proverb reads as follows:

*"When there is no enemy on the inside, there is no enemy outside who can do you any harm."*

I want to take the time to delve on that aphorism a little more because bad stress impacts millions of people within our Western society, and probably billions more globally. Bad stress becomes chronic anxiety that chooses to dwell in our minds and that permanent placement on a daily basis destroys our internal organs over time. For example, good stress increases our cortisol (boosting adrenaline) to promote alertness and to activate our fight-or-flight (run) response defensive mechanism, to survive in perceived dangerous situations. When I was younger, my twin brother and I would get chased by a Doberman Pinscher as we exited our school bus to head home. The owner raised his Doberman to be aggressive and very intimidating. We would jump on and zigzag around cars and jump over fences to find some refuge of protection.

When we arrived to a place of safety from this Doberman, we were absolutely drained of energy, as we expelled some life force out of our vessels. As I ran, I obsessed over "what if" narratives. *What if this Doberman catches up to me, what if I fall, and what if I get tired and stop?* Now, imagine when we obsess over and over about relationships, job promotions, or some other issue within our internal dialogue. What do we think is happening inside of our bodies as our blood pressure and sugar levels constantly spike higher and higher, to provide us with alertness and an instant boost of energy? Cortisol is responsible for more than just our belly fat. Cortisol is responsible for regulating our sleep, our blood pressure, our blood sugar, and inflammation inside and around our joints. When we become consumed with fear, we become consumed with bad stress, causing poor sleep habits and hypertension issues, to name a few. This knowledge does a fabulous job informing us of this serious problem, but it does not have the power to give us courage. And, courage is a requirement to overcome our fears, especially anxiety that dwells from deep within inside us. I struggled with many anxieties, and only I had the power to conquer those anxieties.

Power emerged from my internal soul when I felt the pressure or fear from external pressures; sadly, none of them were physical threats. On the contrary, they were psychological threats; however, I generated quiet courage and action to prevent them from invading and occupying my psyche. Courage requires an action to stop fear in its tracks, placing an intangible injunction on fear's psychological activity and advantage. When we attack life and stay in the flow of its vast energy, we move intently and creatively to spark enough momentum to make fear an obstacle that passes by without judgment. The secret is courage does not take some robust effort; courage needs **deliberate** intent to move the unstoppable train (us) down the tracks to a limitless life. Most people have a fear of the inevitable expiration of life, even though most of us recognize our mortality. Some peoples' fear is too resilient to accept the obvious—death. The beauty of death is that it awaits all of us. Yes, you heard me correctly; death is beautiful because it is part of the natural flow and process of our human existence. I used to wrestle with the fear of death, and many nights, I awoke to a fast heartbeat, heavy breathing, and cold sweats...until one day, I boldly addressed my fear of death. I approached death head on, and I allowed my being to feel all of those intimate emotions that accompany death.

*"Expect nothing, accept everything."* —Michael Bonnell

My courage came when I decided to check my life, and stopped expecting to live forever, as some immortal physical presence. I began to embrace life as is—a brief moment in the physical realm. Mahatma Gandhi's words below inspired my new mantra on my existence:

*"Seek knowledge as if you will live forever. Live life as if you will die tomorrow."*

My accumulated knowledge, life experiences, and paradigm shift motivated me to embrace my future demise, erupting this hidden passion to improve my mind, my body, and my spirit on a daily basis. I did not become morose or saddened by this truth of temporal existing; on the contrary, I became alive and free. Free to be the authentic me and free to be limitless in a world contrived of limitations. Did this mindset shift remove my small fear of the unknown? Not immediately and not completely, but I can proudly say I meet all my small fears with hope and optimism. This approach gives me opportunities to explore my death during my conscious dream state. Courage is needed to picture myself on my death bed. I can vividly picture myself, laughing and asking family members and friends non-serious questions in my hospital room or some unique space in my home. I can see myself urging them to rejoice in my death and my return to eternal and optimal glory. My death dreams are palpable to the point that I can feel my short breaths and heightened anxiousness as my spirit prepares to exit my vessel.

My choice to dream in this manner requires courage and creativity to contrive a corporeal dream of this nature. We will all experience death, so I believe we should all begin to manufacture the necessary courage and creativity to find some level of comfort with our inevitable deaths. The hope is to utilize this momentum to subdue present and future fears while remembering that all fears merely happen in the present moment. When we live with fear, we tap into our inner gods and become creators and originators. (I will discuss inner gods more in the next chapter.) However, we are all creators, and we create something new with every second of every breath we expel from our lungs, whether we acknowledge this reality or not. Phones, cars, clothes, etc. were created by finite beings, even though the inspiration to create derives from our inner guide, our spirits. Our spirits communicate this inner language with the external shell, by using hands, eyes, and other fleshly parts to produce innovate thoughts. Some inner questions led me to my truth and my hidden courage, so I have drafted those three questions to move beyond my fear and to attack fear with boldness.

1.  **Why do we activate our inner courage?**
2.  **How do we activate our inner courage?**
3.  **What role does our courage activation play in our inherent creator?**

When those answers are clearly defined and understood, we will be ready to die to our expectations and to tap into our inner God. I will share my answers to demonstrate the activation process to being limitless. **I activate inner courage because I see it as an opportunity to acquire whatever is on the opposite side of fear. I know that when I walk in courage, it is far greater than succumbing to** my fear. I activate my inner courage by stating, "Check Your Life: Be Limitless," and I act or move towards my fear, mentally or physically. My limitless belief enables me to recognize fear as a prerequisite to creating anything in my physical realm.

If you find it hard to come up with answers to those questions, I encourage you to state the following: **Check Your Life: Be Limitless...I am a limitless spiritual being. I am a creator, and I welcome fear. I use fear to attack life and to create a uniqueness in my personal and professional life.** This statement should be repeated every morning and periodically throughout the day until you start to believe in your individual power to create and to be a unique god in the now.

When those words are stated with authority and belief, we vibrate on a high positive frequency that raises us above our daily frustrations and judgments of this life. We become something greater than a finite being, and we no longer dwell with pointless competition of this life. We walk with a heightened sense of freedom and an elevated state of joy. When this process occurs, we are automatically raised to the level of a spiritual God, who dwells in a physical plane. God is not implied to offend any overtly religious zealots, so I am asking you all to open up to the possibilities of being limitless. Remember, God is used to imply that we are made in perfection and in the image of an almighty God[10] and a part of its universal current.

- What have you utilized your courage for?
- In what ways have you employed creativity and courage to conquer a fear?
- How do you feel when I refer to you as a limitless God? Please expound on your responses.

# Die to Expectations and Tap into Your Inner God

*"Life is the dancer and you are the dance."*
*- Eckhart Tolle*

It is imperative to remember that we are all perfectly made in the image of the supreme intelligence, supreme order, omnipotent presence, or God. Some religions or people refer to this spirit as energy, Chi, God, or themselves. In the Western world, we view God as the Almighty who saved the world in a human form because we want to humanize God. When we humanize something considered infinite and too complicated to understand, it makes us feel more comfortable with accepting an idea of God, our creator. Many Christians combine God and Jesus into one spirit, and once again, I believe many people do this to conceptually view God as human. Yet, God is not human, and our minds are void of an understanding to conceptualize the vastness of this energy, spirit, and infiniteness. I would venture to bet that some Christians are struggling to read the previous sentences, and some might view my words as demonic, heretic, or a form of paganism. We all tend to judge situations, people, and things when they fail to fit into our mental paradigms of understanding. Our expectations keep us tied to our adopted beliefs and labels, limiting us from accessing our personal heavens and from the ability to walk with God and to become a God, instead of our brief moments of godliness (god).

I know my interchangeability of God and god might be creating confusion as you read this book, and I did this to produce confusion and to make you uncomfortable within your disposition. But before I explain, I want you to ask yourself, "why do I feel uncomfortable?" Is it due to some religious upbringing? Is it due to society making God seem untouchable? Or, is it because our inner spirit feels some truth connection to being a God or god at times? Questions lead us to deeper understanding and to unmask our hidden truth. Jesus was considered profound and ahead of his time because he asked questions that challenged the core of one's spirit. "You of little faith, why are you so afraid?[11]" My question is, why are some of us afraid to question our beliefs? There is nothing to be afraid of because what lived in Jesus, Gandhi, Muhammad, Krishna, Lao Tzu, and many other religious seers now dwells obscurely in us, and the only reason it is obscure is due to our lack of belief. We have the propensity to use our conscious decisions to embrace fear and to reject belief.

Once again, why are we so afraid to refer to ourselves as a God or god? We need to cogitate this question without immediately subconsciously rejecting any truth in being a God or god. Some religious people have said that God, our all-loving spirit, will strike them down with vengeance for believing in this fashion. I urge you to read my following sentences with an open mind, spirit, and heart. Please consider some "what if" possibilities to what I am referring to. Before I explain further, let's discuss my interpretation and/or expression of a God or god. My interpretation of a God in the physical realm is someone who found heaven on Earth by living in contentment, joy, righteousness, and who strived for constant spiritual, mental, and physical evolution. This constant and consistent pursuit changes this sentient being into a limitless soul who flows along an esoteric path and dwells in perfect peace. These God individuals have freed themselves from the trappings and distractions of this world and walk with absolute or infinite bliss, removing their old masks and replacing those masks with that of their spiritual creator, to become a walking creation. Yet, a god with a lowercase "g" is someone who touches heaven sometimes or in temporal states, but lacks the intent and belief to live in this state permanently, as a lifestyle. For example, they may have contentment, joy, righteousness, and strive for continuous financial evolution to serve the less fortunate or impoverished; but they lack the intent in their spiritual and physical journey. The beauty of gods is seen every day, in music, sports, educators, spiritual advisors, etc., but they might lack the belief of having a healthy body or a quality marriage or relationships with family and friends.

A God with a capital "G" is someone whole (complete) who believes he or she is limitless and has the spirit to acquire the best body, sharpest mind, and an ascension in spirit. An ascension that enables a God to acquire esoteric wisdom from the spiritual realm, to manifest things on the physical plane. Gods walk with a heightened belief every day, even when they fall short of some personal accomplishment; they continue to walk with intent and absolute belief. The only way to walk into this glory, to taste this heaven, and to tap into this inner God is to shift our minds from an external motivation to a constant internal inspiration. A quiet knowing comes from within us, causing us to Check our Lives and to be limitless to our pursuits of authentic voices (voice of God). When we sit still, we have an inner voice that encourages us, inspires us, and leads us to believe beyond our proverbial beliefs. We will inevitably tap into our inner God when we choose to follow infinite intelligence, making the contrived expectations of others wither and die.

Buddha stated that expectations are a form of suffering because we are desiring something, someone, or some idea that does not exist rather than being content with the present moment—the only moment that ever existed. Consider some of my past personal expectations and consider the dangers of those past expectations. I expected to be 6'5" tall, so I could play in the NBA...but I only grew to be 5'7½". I always add the half, but I might actually be a little shorter, according to a past professional football workout. I was listed as 5'6" with my shoes off, but I walk around with shoes on; so I prefer 5'7½". Two expectations never materialized: I never grew close to that height, and I never made millions dunking a basketball professionally in the NBA. What if I became consumed with grief due to these failed expectations? I probably would have created some level of perpetual suffering, and this would have produced a personal hell for me, with a personal cell and psychological chains to anchor me to that pit of hell. Many people I know tend to struggle with this offered notion to die to expectations because they perceived it as dying to a creation of personal goals.

I contest that my idea of dying to expectations is slightly different. For example, I established a goal to read 60 books during the start of 2019, so I was constantly read, anywhere between three and five books each month. Yet, I was not married to this goal; instead, I was inspired by this goal, with no true expectations of reaching it. If I had failed to read 60 books, I would not have suffered in a personal hell. On the contrary, I would still have been content reading any number of books because I fell in love with the process of reading rather than the set outcome. The power of my stated goal of 60 books surely inspired my inner God to read. I never reached my goal of 60 books, but I did read 55 books in 2019. My goal pushed me beyond the average number of most Americans—which is 12 books a year, according to research. Another thing to consider is that our stated goals derive from some internal inspiration rather than some external motivation from another finite being. Our God lies dormant and waits for us to claim its power, but the sad part is that many people die every second and never tap into this dormant power. I heard Les Brown capturing this reality very vividly and beautifully in one of his many inspiring stories about a dying man who had visitors prior to his death. The visitors informed the dying man that they were his gifts and opportunities that he never tapped into and used, and now they must die with him and be lost forever, to this physical world. This story conjures two pertinent thoughts. Firstly, we are all brought to this planet from a higher source, and we are brought here to do something no other God was instructed to do. Secondly, I am afraid I may stand before my creator and my creator may stretch out their infinite and metaphorical arms and say, "I wanted you to do so much more, but you decided to do much less," as he or she pinches his or her index finger and thumb together to demonstrate my small efforts. I live to leave no stone unturned, so I can never fall into social comparison. When we dwell in that world, we live by conditions and expectations. I live limitless, so my competition and comparison is only with self.

Most Gods do not believe the almighty or supreme being (God) does not hold the form of any finite being or human, and I would not disagree. My view inspires me and does not come from other finite thinking, and my view does not care about other finite judgments from those sentient beings. Peoples' expectations and judgments no longer anchor me to attempt to gain their approval because I choose to embrace the opposite of this conditioned fear and to live a limitless life. A life where death is normal, and the present moment is our only reality. What are some of your expectations? How do your expectations inspire you? How do your expectations hold you back from being limitless? What will you do to die to your set expectations and expectations from other people?

# Live a Limitless Life: Gratefulness Attracts Abundance

*"Turn your wounds into wisdom."*
*~ Oprah Winfrey*

We all have the power of free will. Choices were given to us at birth. We were all born limitless until limited-minded beings presented us with some very convincing conditions that stripped us of our innocence and trained us to a more limited way of thinking. At first, they were small and somewhat trivial limitations, stemming from the way we should stand, sit, eat, run, and engage in random activities. These innocuous conditions taught us subtly to seek a right way to live, to think, to act, to speak, etc. from someone older and perceived wiser than us. The significant issue with this previous statement is that children tend to have more fun and joy than these wise elders. We need to think long and hard about the previous sentences because many of us are comfortable with conditions, even if they do not make sense. I was repeatedly told I needed to mature and to start "acting my age," whatever that means. I never figured out how to act at 10, 20, 30, or 40 years of age. Like really, how are we supposed to act? This is another form of judgment and labelling which does not conform to some suspected way to govern ourselves. Yet, when I embraced the idea of being a God, I realized there is never a true, set way to act. The trick is we must decide to be in the now and to experience life as is, with no expectations. On the flipside, when we govern ourselves according to others' opinions, we hijack ourselves to their finite ideologies. We should expect nothing and embrace everything if we intend to live a limitless life.

When we live with this power, our attitudes default to positions of gratitude and contentment. I would also argue that this positive mind shift leads to a more abundant life. Jesus, the dominant figure in Christianity, wanted to offer us a more abundant life, a life that shatters chains and manmade limitations[12]. Most people limit themselves by living under privileged or unrealistic expectations. For example, many of us live as though simply breathing and experiencing life are guarantees, even though millions of people die every day. We are gifted with life, in every present moment. We are each like a speck of dust, and eventually, we all will blow away. This understanding of a temporal existence should spark us to a measure of gratefulness, enabling us to reject our limited perspectives. It forced me to ask, "Why do I waste any of my precious moments complaining, when I could be using that energy to present solutions?" When I embraced the fact that today could possibly be my last day, it allowed me to live and to accept the now as the only option. I do not consider the possibly I would be given another day, another week, or another year. I become mindful of every second and accept it could be my last. The fragility of time bestows me with the power needed to seize the day. As I awake each morning, I quietly say, "Check Your Life: Today might be my last day, and it will be the best day of my life."

This new mantra represents what Andy Dufresne meant by the quote in the movie, *Shawshank Redemption*, "Get busy living or get busy dying." Once I make the conscious decision to take control of the day, I treat myself kindly with three things I am grateful for early in the morning, just like we talked about in a previous chapter when I outlined my daily routine. This begins my off with positive emotions and an inspired purpose. I find simple—but personally important—things to be grateful for, such as an opportunity to speak in front of my students; or even something as major as being able to inhale and exhale without any complications. Many of us are blessed with the opportunity to breathe freely and expressively without any issues, but we take this process for granted. When we live limitless, we understand the importance of all our blessings, taking nothing for granted. We all have been gifted with the power to live limitless and to attract abundance, in some form or fashion. The key to unlock our doors of abundance is to find gratefulness with every breath. A grateful attitude should be followed by a concentrated effort to acknowledge all facets of that breath which would lead us to mindfulness.

Mindfulness is required to appreciate every breath, and we do that by aligning our minds, bodies, and spirits to that given moment of breathing. When we are unable to be mindful and to be grateful in these three important pillars (mind, body, and spirit), we will be unable to obtain a limitless life. However, we furnish poverty when we are deficit in any one of those pillars. I am not referring to our financial state or money because money is just a resource anyway; money does not hold any value for the individual spirit of man or woman. Poverty is considered the state of being inferior in quality or an inadequate amount of something. I have witnessed people who are impoverished financially, but who are extremely wealthy in their spiritual being. Poverty tends to attack all pillars when we buy into labels, attacking individuals' minds and spirits, and eventually, their bodies. Many people allow their impoverished lives to ruin their relationships with other sentient beings when relationship formation should be a natural process. We were created to be interdependent beings, who share love and experiences with each other. We seem to forgotten this authentic connection, using technology to form and to sustain our relationships. We have transformed into technological objects, who measure our importance in Facebook likes and Twitter retweets. Where are the genuine connections and love? A limitless life cannot and will not derive from our social media existence.

This message is not coming from a technophobic or techno-ignorant individual; I deleted my Instagram when I had over 20k followers because I wanted to go in a new direction, only having organic and authentic followers. Many people utilize social media as their modality to communicate and to build fictitious relationships with other people or bots. These methods hijack our personal and intimate connections, to transition us from real beings into subjective objects. When this occurs in our relationships, we tend to lose a sliver of our richness and truth. This deficit is filled with limited happiness that is found in instant likes from a picture on Facebook or Instagram, or direct messages through Snapchat. People live like-to-like for temporal happiness, very similar to people living paycheck-to-paycheck for survival. Relationships relying solely on likes are really only several likes away from poverty and heartache. I witness college students and adults getting upset because specific people have not liked their pictures in a timely fashion—or liked the picture at all. Reliance on others to like our comments or pictures for happiness creates a type of abundance that needs to be received externally and processed internally for a modicum of happiness. This process is contingent on external power and constructed for eventual failure; this is a flawed system. Relationships were chosen as my poverty example because we were designed to interact and to unconditionally love one another. All of our enjoyable pleasures are created by other sentient beings, through some production process or some service deliverable.

There are countless research articles that emphasize the importance of intimate relationships. Yet, I believe individuals need to bring their truth to create intimate relationships, and we do that by bringing our best mind, body, and spirit engagement. Below, I will attempt to demonstrate the pivotal role of a limitless mind, spirit, and body; and the aggregate of those elements is influential and authoritative power toward supplying us with gratefulness and abundant lives. A limitless mind is a mind that transcends all constructed labels and lies that originated from the Tree of Knowledge.

For example, I identify with many labels, but I hold no attachments or beliefs to those labels. I have a vocation as an educator, and I identify as male and a black man due to census bureau statistics. Remember, power comes from the belief in an identity. Racist and prejudice ideologies are birthed from strong attachments or beliefs to manmade labels, with finite meanings. I know some of you are rolling your eyes and might be bloviating about how proud you are to claim your race, ethnic group, and/or gender. I get it. I thought along the same vein for decades. Yet, I want you to ask yourself, what do those labels mean? Do they make you more special? Do they give you power over your situations or your life circumstances? Do they give you the right to exclude others with different opinions or different appearances? Whatever our answers appear to be, our answers will eventually die with us when we can no longer produce another breath and no longer create in our time and space, known as the true law of relativity.

When our minds shift from limited attachments, we can consistently perform limitless actions. Our minds and bodies should be seen as a concomitant with our spirits. Thoughts and actions should align to supply us with the most limitless rote behaviors. Putting the labels in my life to death furnished a rebirth to limitless power in my actions. In 2011, I was playing semiprofessional football as a running back with the Des Moines Blaze in Des Moines, Iowa. During the last game of the season and prior to our league playoff run, I was diagnosed with peroneal nerve damage, better known as foot drop. My left foot and toes were paralyzed, and I lost the ability to run. We were headed into the playoffs as the frontrunners for a national championship, but the doctor told me I would be unable to play, and maybe unable to feel sensation in my left foot for several years. I was in excruciating pain, but the pain did not make me mad, just slightly frustrated. This unique pain humbled me and heightened my awareness towards gratefulness, acknowledging it could have been much worse and recognizing some people had it much worse.

> *I complained about having no shoes until I met a man who had no feet.*
> *- Persian proverb*

I saw this as an opportunity to tap into my inner God and to see if my limitless power truly existed, or if the law of attraction was merely sound rhetoric.

Every night, and throughout each day, I visualized myself sprinting with the team and clutching the football in my right hand. Those visions were so robust that I spoke with sound confidence, "Check Your Life: Be Limitless...I am healthy, and I will play in our final championship game." My words would inspire me, and I would challenge my physical self to run outside every day until I lost my balance and fell to the ground. I never got upset, though, and I never stopped believing my inner God would respond to this challenge. I knew I would run and play in our championship game, and I expected to run well. On August 22, 2011, I ran the ball 67 yards and averaged 6.7 yards per tote in that championship game. I ran well, as I believed I would. And, we beat the Midwest Rampage 41-10, to win our first national championship. I proudly wear our championship ring around my neck because it is a sign of the limitless power that transcended my mental and physical selves, raising me above my diagnosis. When we are limitless in our spirits, it is easier to witness our unlimited potentials in our minds and bodies. I spoke about limitlessness in our minds and bodies because they activate limitlessness in our spirits. As we continue to operate with limitless spirits, we remain in the present moment and live limitless as a God, with abundant joy. This joy enables us to operate with the power needed to find contentment in all situations and to function from a neutral stance.

Our joy conjures up gratefulness and attracts an abundance of limitless opportunities to grow and to be at peace with the internal limitlessness in ourselves. This gives us the limitless power needed to repudiate the opinions and judgments of those we choose to share our experiences with. We understand validation comes from our spiritual being and not from finite beings. This enabled me to see and to feel God deep inside of myself, so I began to realize my God dwells inside me and I became this perfect image of my God. This heightened notion of my authentic being led me to be more selfish and to be more committed to being a service to my creator of energy and giver of flesh. I knew I needed to focus on employing my gifts to be of service, rather than to placate the ideals and judgments of other finite beings.

- In what ways do you limit your finite being?
- What ideologies are stopping you from believing you are the pure essence of God?
- What makes you afraid to believe in your inner God or your greater form?

# Be Selfish: Be Willing to Risk Everything for Your Purpose

*"The wise man does not lay up his own treasures. The more he gives to others, the more he has for his own."*

*~ Lao Tzu*

Selfishness is perceived by many people in Western society as a negative character trait, even though, one can argue that selfishness is permeated throughout majority of the Western culture. I will attempt to redefine this word, so we can glean its limitless power and construct a more factual understanding of my belief on being selfish. Being selfish means to put one's purpose or self-first. To love one's self unconditionally and unapologetically ends up being the crux of the word selfish. When we live from this selfish perspective, we must be willing to risk everything for the greater good of our purpose and/or reason for existing in our physical dispositions. It sounds simple, but this way of being is far from a simple way to live, in today's culture. I would argue that most people live contrary to my definition and belief of being selfish, and I would also state that many people probably oppose my desire for people to be more selfish. Many people spend boundless energy bragging about being selfless, bloviating about how they put others' needs before their own, and about how they always put other people first. I have heard many people express excitedly how much they love their kids, parents, friends, or lovers more than themselves. I have always felt vastly disconnected from these statements, even as a child, even when I fathered my own kids.

Every airline in the United States discusses what airline passengers should do if cabin failure occurs during a flight. Flight attendants stand in front of passengers and demonstrate how they should don a mask to mitigate the loss of oxygen during cabin failure. However, the caveat is that the passenger must don and secure their mask first, prior to helping any other passenger, even if the passenger is a relative. We must provide safety to ourselves first. I support this selfish notion, and it should be applied in our practical lives. We must treat our precious seconds with the same sense of urgency as airplanes that experience cabin failure; we must live limitless lives first. I know this must sound cruel and heartless to some, because we enjoy eating that fruit from the Tree of Knowledge that informs us to put others first. Once again, I have always rejected this harmful fruit. Understanding that every great thing has an origin—and if love's origin is God or supreme intelligence—how can we skip ourselves and give greater love to a third source or human being in this matter? We must love ourselves unconditionally before we can love others unconditionally; we must stay connected to the first source, this supreme intelligence and abundant love. This order demands selfish commitment to love one's self, a love that goes beyond our internal condemnations and external judgments. This pursuit is a difficult one, due to our conditioned desire to interact and to serve others prior to serving ourselves.

We are conditioned to be selfless and to perceive selfish behavior as an ill-gotten or egregious form of behavior. I can still remember how my mother would encourage me to share my video games and my toys with my brothers and friends—"be fair and share with your brothers" became a common theme in my home environment. My parents were not the only people reverberating this message. Many relatives uttered the same rhetoric, and even teachers encouraged me to share blocks and LEGOS with other kids during play time. Those adults were probably taught the same lessons, and those lessons were taught out of love. Some people are afraid that being selfish would lead to an isolated existence. And, what parent or loved one would want someone they love to have to deal with an isolated existence? Our loved ones raise us out of fear, so they are sharing this information to protect us from external harm. Remember, our parents were told the same stories we were told, even though it felt natural to put themselves first. They were conditioned to share first, and schools reinforced this idea to share first.

School is an institution of rules, instructing us to be docile or submissive to policies and order. Individuals were born to be free, so our innate spirits are not receptive to policies and rules. Most policy makers and leaders in the so-called 'free' society tend to follow or claim Christianity as their religion, an acceptable and safe label for our Westernized culture. Yet, most leaders coerce (and even intimidate) people to follow these manmade rules, such as religion. Forgetting that Jesus's sole purpose was to free people from Roman rules, many theological scholars can argue that Jesus was a habitual rule breaker. Being selfish is designed to redirect us back to our inherent natures and visceral instincts, and towards Jesus's way of living. My words are written to present an alternative truth to manmade rules, and my shared truth shall set us free—free to explore the truth that lies deep within all of us—because at the end of the day, my words are just my words, and are maybe not your truth. When I followed this system of rules, I rebelled and condemned myself to bondage, as I continuously fell short of society's expectations; expectations that became my family's expectations and my personal expectations.

As previously discussed, our power emerges when we die to expectations and come alive to our limitless design. We need to understand that it is time for us to reclaim our limitless power by placing ourselves before others. The greatest commands from Jesus were, "'Love the Lord your God with all your heart and with all your soul and with all your mind.' This is the first and greatest commandment. And the second is like it: 'Love your neighbor as yourself'"[13]. We should evaluate this statement more critically, with an introspective probe deep into our spiritual being. We must become unconditionally loving to ourselves, to touch our inner God, and we must utilize all of that love to others from the depths of our subconscious and conscious thoughts. This is my paraphrased version of the greatest commandment, and it is void of pleasing others and capitulating to all their agreements and expectations. The second commandment is to love your neighbor as you first choose to establish unconditional love for yourself. This scripture is the epitome of being selfish, and I surmise that these commandments scream out for us to be more selfish, in order to satisfy God and our inner God, which comes from this supreme intelligence, life, and energy.

Without this heightened satisfaction to our creator and inner God, we will lack the power required to unapologetically be selfish and to risk it all. Being selfish taught me how to love myself and, in turn, it taught me how to authentically love others from a genuine stance. When I performed a self-assessment and completed an introspective look, I realized my selfless approach to life accompanied a deeper need for validation. I longed to fit in and to belong to people whom I respected and looked up to; and if they did not approve of my attitudes and actions, I felt unloved and condemned. This disapproval of myself created a self-hate of myself. I only loved and felt great about myself when my parents or respected individuals gave me a positive compliment, motivating me to love myself with some very limited conditions. One night, I asked myself a question, "Why am I still unhappy?" This question came after I had already acquired a comfortable lifestyle and a plethora of successes, in and out of my proverbial professions. I still felt a deep-seated void within my physical being.

However, as I slept that night, I was visited by a ghostly spirit, in a very vivid dream. This powerful spirit took me back to two impactful encounters as a young child. The first encounter occurred when I was about two or three years old, as I laid quietly on the floor of my mother's mobile home in the quiet town of Stantons-burg, NC. I heard hushed chatter between my mother and cousin, and my cousin moved toward me, motioning me to be quiet, raising her index finger to her lips. Then I heard her say to my mother, "It is Richard, their daddy is outside." I felt an uneasiness and wondered, *why should I fear my daddy?* And for whatever reason I thought, *Am I good enough for my daddy?* All of a sudden, I heard a voice quietly say, "I am here, and I've always been here; all you need is me." I felt instant peace and a hint of selfishness, as if this inner voice mattered more than any other noise, I had previously heard about myself and any other opinions from others. That peace transitioned me to another past encounter, and this time I was at my aunt's house while my cousins and I played school in one of her back rooms. Suddenly, her doorbell rang and, after several seconds of some shuffling around from my aunt and mother, my aunt sprinted to the back and hushed us to silence.

I heard my mother and aunt converse that Richard was here to give us a TV for Christmas, but we were not permitted to see him. To this day, I am not privy to the reason; yet, I was privy to my inner feeling of rejection and my inner feeling of being inadequate. This time, I asked myself, *why am I not loved by my daddy?* My inner voice grew stronger than the previous voice and stated the following with veracity: "I love you, and my love is greater than any other love. Never look to anyone else for love, I live in you; and I will always live in you and love you. You will never need anyone or anything to ever validate you again in your lifetime." When I awoke from my sleep, I knew the authentic voice of validation and power lived on the inside of me. This led me to listen to the voice within and to focus on pleasing the voice within and to never look outside for validation ever again. I became selfish and obsessed with loving myself first, with no preset conditions. We can only be willing to risk it all when we unconditionally love ourselves first.

- What is your greatest love?
- How do you view yourself in comparison to the love of others?
- How do you see selfishness benefiting your life, personally and professionally?
- What would be some of the greatest challenges to your pursuit of being selfish?
- Please create a story of a selfish life that gives you a limitless existence.

# Be Unconditional Love and Find Peace in All Situations

*"Nobody can bring you peace but yourself."*
*~ Ralph Waldo Emerson*

Conditions have become a normal part of our lives. It is seen as an automatic framing of our human condition. Conditions are the foundation or the crux of our labels; labels originate from the Tree of Knowledge. When conditions are subconsciously and consciously applied to our lives, they serve as countless limitations in our lives. And those limitations stifle our abilities to love unconditionally and rationally, in my humble opinion. In order to foster unconditional love, we must be willing to remain optimistic and search for something positive in all situations within our lives. This paradigm shifts us away from conditional love to a more systematic way to love in unfavorable situations. This new method produces universal peace and acceptance of diversity while also promoting inclusion of all people and situations deemed different. Some people might argue that this new method produces universal meekness and weakness. However, the perception does not matter to me because labels do not exist to a limitless being. Now, I am that limitless being—we are those limitless beings. I will humbly submit to any subjective label, as long as it leads me to universal peace of all mankind. Peace comes from our ability to find contentment with all situations, and this peace is available to all of us, in all situations.

Contentment is our guiding path towards unconditional love. My arduous journey to unconditional love has been one of the hardest pursuits of my young existence. But, the acquisition of unconditional love has been the most rewarding and most powerful weaponry added to my robust and limitless spirit. My focus was to love as Jesus did when he carried his cross to his crucifixion and said, "Father, forgive them, for they do not know what they are doing"[14]. I repeatedly asked to acquire unconditional love, so I can proactively love all people, even my enemies, without any conditions. Then, I said, "Check Your Life: Be limitless, I am unconditional love."

In 2014, my parents and I had a disagreement, and this disagreement led to a contentious relationship for about four years. I will share this story from my inappropriate actions and to demonstrate how we have the ability to take control and to love from an unconditional perspective, regardless of the situation; it is always a choice. Family conflict can create chronic stress and extreme resentment within all parties involved. So, I write this from my own personal experience and in no way does it reflect my parents' thoughts and/ or opinions.

To start with, I would feel a sense of uneasiness in my stomach and a pinch of shakiness in my body when my parents' names were brought up, or I saw their names on my phone's caller ID. I had a strong disdain for them, and I would tell some family members and friends how I felt, bringing a lot of inner pain and hate to increase the venom in my words. It was all negative—my thoughts, my actions, and my collective inner energy. My love was tied to this negative condition, stopping all unconditional love and destroying all peace within my spiritual, mental, and physical domain. I was immobilized by my self-generated pain and hatred. I had no peace within my spirit, so I had no peace in my flesh. I constructed an enemy within, and I fed this enemy all the things I disliked about them and all the things I deemed 'bad' about them, not knowing I was hating and killing myself in the process. When we hate others, we end up hating ourselves.

Unconditional love and limitless beings do not fraternize with hate because they are incapable of associating with that opposing force. My enemy grew stronger as I thought more and more about their actions, and I grew restless, conjuring up troubling dreams in my subconscious and agitating thoughts in my conscious state. I could not move beyond my conditional love for them, and I consumed myself with judgment and hate. Eventually, I realized my limited conditions correlated to limited conditions I created for myself, and my personal judgment for them became a personal judgment for myself. I was a wretched man who was in need of unconditional love, but this unconditional love could not come from my parents or any external object or person outside of my spiritual being. I learned that unconditional love could only come from within myself, and not from any other being or so-called positive circumstance. Once I turned the mirror away from them and aimed it squarely at myself, I was able to clearly see the huge log of judgment and conditional love in my own eyes.

I was able to love myself unconditionally and freely, with no attachments to other people's opinions and judgments. When my mind shifted, I shifted my focus to gratefulness and things that I deemed 'good.' I accepted my parents for simply being my parents, and I died to any perceived expectations or preconceived judgments about them. I was able to remember and to focus on the positive times: the times my parents showed up to my PTA meetings, my school events, and my sporting events. This left me feeling joyful and at peace. I was able to ruminate over the pleasant times my father tucked me into bed at night and told me how proud he was to adopt us and be our father. I produced moments of nostalgia, generating the feelings of my mother rubbing my chest and giving me medicine when I was sick and too weak to leave my bed. I felt universal peace, and I understood the power of unconditional love from my generated moments of gratefulness. I tasted the sweet love of Jesus, of Buddha, of Muhammad, and of my God deep inside of me. All notable spirits live deep within all of us, but we must believe to receive this omnipotent presence. Our soils must be fertile before we can plant seers' and sages' spirits deep on the inside and prior to receiving our inner peace. Unconditional love is the sole requirement needed to produce fertile soil in our lives. Our lives provide us with myriad opportunities to practice unconditional love, and it is our job to raise our awareness to recognize those positive opportunities.

My opportunities presented themselves every time I debated with a family member over their opinions, or became impatient while driving my car through busy traffic. Standing in chaotic convenient store lines have provided opportunities to become aware of my emotions. How do we react during frustrating situations? Verbally or nonverbally? How do we feel? These uncomfortable moments present us with a chance to rise above those conditions, by using unconditional love to experience the moment and to suspend judgment. This unconditional love places us in the position to calmly pick apples from the Tree of Life while operating in the present moment; this is an absolute state of contentment and peace. Raising kids and working provide me with circumstances to be mindful and to choose unconditional love while functioning in situations that can tempt me to be frustrated. During my son's senior football season, I had to witness his coaches constantly overlooking him, even as he led the team in rushing yardage and kick return yardage. One coach would deliberately taunt him and challenge him, and his coach's actions infuriated me until I decided to place aside my emotions and act with unconditional love. I reminded my son that life was not fair and that it was never designed to be fair. I reminded him how unfair it was when he was the star in track and field, and how some of his teammates had to watch and to support him run and win in multiple sprinting events.

I also reminded him that life is designed to challenge us, and that our character is developed when we are treated unkindly and still choose to love those individuals who treat us inappropriately. As hard as it was to choose unconditional love when my son was treated in that fashion, I chose to pray for his coaches and to wish them peace and happiness, regardless of their unfair treatment. It was extremely hard to do, but the more I acted with unconditional love, the more unconditional love filled my spiritual essence. Sometimes, our proactive actions can invoke unconditional love when we cannot find that love and peace in our minds. This has taught me to do more and to talk less. When we act in this manner, we are telling our spirits that we believe, even in spite of our stubborn minds. Life gives us these trial runs, hopefully to prepare us for our major tests as we journey through life. One of my major tests came as I submitted my dossier for tenure and promotion as a college professor. A former graduate student made an allegation against me on November 15, 2019, claiming I stole her research. Initially, I was shocked and angered by this baseless allegation, and I seethed with hate for about two days. As I sulked around my house and played the victim, a quiet voice said to me, "Check your life and be limitless, bro." I chuckled to myself and felt an instant sense of joy.

I walked to the bathroom mirror and told myself, "Check Your Life: Be limitless, this is a great situation and the universe is doing something major for me, be patient and stop complaining." Little did I know how powerful and how true that statement would become for me. After that quiet voice, I stopped speaking negatively about the situation and wished the complainant peace and joy, from a genuine place in my heart and in my sentient spirit. While I was being filled in my spirit, my cup began to overflow with abundant joy. Then, on November 27, 2019, I received a notice from this former student's lawyer, asking me to stop any future publications of her work. This was a typical lawyer scare tactic, but this time I felt nothing and recognized the power of the universe, knowing something major was about to happen in my life. I believed deep in my heart that the universe was working desperately on my behalf. Two hours later, I received an email from the department of veteran's affairs, stating my claim to discharge my student loans was approved on November 15, 2019 and sent to the department of education on November 26, 2019. My $100,000 student loan debt was paid in full, so the universe was working on my behalf as this ordeal was going on. The beauty is that my gratefulness was more abundant due to the allegation by my former graduate student. I can honestly say, I am extremely grateful to this former student and offer love and peace to her. This unconditional love has set me free and placed me in a perpetual state of peace. This perpetual peace led me to a limitless power that worked in the unseen world on my behalf.

I chose to rise up and be a hero rather than succumb to the powerless state of being a helpless victim. When we complain to others and blame life for our many problems, we become victims, individuals standing on an isolated island, waiting for some savior to come with a bigger boat. "Life can only be understood backwards; but it must be lived forward" (Soren Kierkegaard). Every time in our past we have failed, every time we felt like life betrayed us, and every time we believed we needed someone to save us; it was life's unconditional way of loving us. Life loved us enough to build an inner resolve and to develop the fortitude and wherewithal to rise above any limited situation, with a limitless power.

- What do you love unconditionally?
- If it is not yourself, why does that thing or that person hold more value when compared to you?
- If it is yourself, how do you demonstrate your unconditional love to yourself, mentally, physically, and spiritually?

# Every Victim Needs a Savior

*"Stop making excuses. Stop being a victim. Take personal responsibility."*
~ *David Goggins*

A victim is an individual who has been harmed or attacked in a given event. A victim is vulnerable and lacks the ability to protect themselves from harm or imminent danger in many situations. A victim is an individual incapable of or unwilling to fight back. Sadly, there are many unfortunate victims in today's societies, and I would argue that the assaults or attacks are mainly unwarranted and unpreventable. Yet, most victims have designed self-imposed sanctions and psychological wars that have impeded them from living a limitless life and left them consuming fruit from the Tree of Knowledge, eating lie after lie until they are left full of self-doubt and self-victimization. I hear my loved ones and friends complaining about people rejecting them and judging them; but more importantly, I hear them judging and hating themselves.

Some of my loved ones boldly articulate their insignificant existence as a result of not having a job that makes some perceived impact in our society. Some people debate the seeming invisibility of their actions and attitudes positively impacting others because they do not receive any immediate gratification (e.g., recognition from people and/or some governing body). Self-hatred is the greatest enemy to people, as they conspicuously grow an enemy within. As this enemy grows, external enemies acquire more power. These two powers (internal and external) become all-consuming, and they destroy our mental, physical, and spiritual advantages within the physical realm. Ultimately, we subject ourselves to becoming helpless victims, enslaved to our negativity, to self-hate, and to "can't do" mentalities. When we transform into this type of victim, we live pessimistic lives and buy into Murphy's Law, a law that indicates when something bad happens, another bad situation tends to follow, creating a snowball effect. We tend to throw ourselves pity parties, sitting around with people who agree with this poor spirit and poor attitude, so we all fester more negatively towards the situation.

We might even eat unhealthy food, get drunk, or engage in some recreational drugs, as we blame our parents, our teachers, our societies, our religious leaders, our politicians, etc. for our poor decisions or uninspired lives. This is one of the greatest distractions that hides in the form of a lie that we tell ourselves. We lie about the true "en-emy" because we turn anything external to our physical container of our spirits into our enemy. The Latin prefix en- means "in," so this indicates that the enemy was never an outside foe; the true enemy has always been the "inner me." This true enemy is our limitless spirit which becomes limited by our generated lies. Lies enter our minds as thoughts, and those thoughts become lies when we act on those thoughts with emotions or beliefs. We consume label after label when we operate in our victim state and when we transform thoughts to lies.

The following are some notable labels: *I am not good enough, I am not smart enough, I did not grow up in the proper neighborhood, my biological father did not love me, and nobody cares about me.*

Lie, lie, lie, lie, and lie—and all void of power until we agree and decide to believe in those labels. Notice, all of those lies started with self-descriptors and the agreement and the decision to regain power over those labels begin with those same descriptors, including the word "I." "I" am the enemy and the one who has limited my power, but also, "I" am the hero who can reclaim my limitless power to remove my mask of lies. When we decide to stop eating fruit from the Tree of Knowledge and to start eating fruit from the Tree of Life, we consciously decide to become limitless and wear our superhero capes during our finite physical existence. Real superheroes are individuals who decide to pursue personal journeys and travel roads less taken.

The famous book, *The Heroes Journey* by Joseph Campbell, discusses the hero's threshold of adventure. When we start our hero's journey, we receive a **call to adventure**, we face **tests/trials**, and we have our great **return**. The author carefully demonstrates how all religious leaders, famous world leaders or sages, and superheroes journeyed through those same three phases prior to their great awakening. Campbell's book did an excellent job explaining the importance of every stage in the evolution process to our great awakening and towards the pursuit of a limitless life. I will give a brief explanation of those three phases, and their connection to becoming a hero. I will also employ some personal stories to prove their power.

A **call to adventure** is when our norms no longer feel authentic and natural, and the victim no longer believes what they has been fed all of their life. The victim decides to explore and to venture out for the truth, and they begin to question everything that they were once conditioned to believe. Once the victim remains on this journey, they become a David Goggins kind of human superhero, becoming *Uncommon Amongst the Common*. David's book does an excellent job highlighting his call to adventure; he once weighed over 300 pounds and engaged in self-hatred until he decided he wanted to re-gain his life and become a Navy SEAL.

Every decision has a consequence; or another way to state this declaration is that every action causes a reaction. When we embark on these new adventures and do something different, we will face **tests/trials**. These **tests/trials** are never easy and require great commitment and effort to overcome. During this period, hostility, delusion, and desire come to life within the hero. We face conflict with family members and friends; we question our abilities to make substantial change; and we discover our limitless abilities to take charge of our lives. Once we pass these tests, we are presented with an opportunity to **return**. Here is an example of this return.

A young man, who was considered a loser in high school because he dropped out and spent some time in drug rehabilitation centers, rose above his 'loser' label and became a success story. This young man went on to believe he was chosen to **return** to his place of greatness in his home, so he could come back to save others from their internal and external enemies and to share the truth, to set others free. This young man and other heroes at the **return** phase believed they had the magical power to influence others and to teach them how to save themselves. We become modern-day alchemists when we become limitless, transitioning from believing to *knowing* our power and its boundless limits. Alchemist were known for transforming matter with their magical powers and creating an elixir, which was known for transforming matter into gold.

Personally, I became an alchemist by transforming my self-hatred and my past poor decisions into personal and professional strategies for worldly successes. Yet, my **call to adventure** began when I was deep within a victim state, thinking the world owed me something and treated me unfairly. I felt like my college football coaches favored other running backs over myself, my college professors sought to fail me, and other people sought to hate me. At this time, I decided to show up late and high (on weed or cannabis) to football practices, I stopped going to class, and I frequently carried a loaded pistol to night clubs. Everything came to a head when I tried to shoot someone in Durham, NC, in February of 1999. My self-hatred transformed into a limited hatred for others, and my inner enemy became an uncontrollable enemy to others. When I looked in the mirror one morning after this incident, I no longer accepted the label of being a thug and of being a loser. I set out on a journey to travel an uncommon path from my set of friends engaged in gang and criminal activity. I sought a path divergent from violence and a world of negativity; I had to be *uncommon amongst the common*, as David Goggins passionately stated, "I wanted to become the baddest mother f%@ker to ever live."

I joined the United States Air Force, and I divorced the notion of being a thug, being a black man, being a Christian, being an athlete, being a limited being, being a victim, and more importantly, being a label. "Check Your Life: Be limitless," and do not be bound to any manmade labels. I am a limitless spirit, and I am made in the perfect image of God. This alone solidifies our limitless existence. I will live an abundant existence, an existence free of stress and worldly labels. I questioned all of my assigned roles and adopted labels, and I soon realized they do not exist when I choose to eat fruit from the Tree of Life. My decision to journey away from my imposed spiritual, physical, and mental beliefs put me at odds with other family members, friends, and people choosing to walk down the comfortable path. This is a path filled with many believers, and this is a path filled with many people afraid of living in the unknown. **Tests/trials** were aplenty in my life, and I failed to overcome many of those self-created obstacles. Every time I failed, those same **tests/trials** reappeared until I was able to pass the test, mentally. Remember, the war is won in the eyes, not the actions. This part of the process is pivotal to us transforming into limitless beings and becoming Gods. Gods live above the fray, and Gods live above emotions and actions that are tied to thoughts. I thought I needed the validation of other people (e.g., parents, opposite sex, perceived respectable people, and family members and friends). Every time I failed to receive validation, I adopted hate and produced an inappropriate judgment of myself. When I stopped investing my spirit, mind, and body into other peoples' opinions, and decided to accept my so-called flaws and so-called strengths as perfection, I passed these **tests/trials** and proceeded to my path of personal truth. A truth that valued my internal character over any external reputation and judgments.

My truth led me to my personal freedom, and I learned my "why" —my reason for existing in this physical plane, and my purpose for "how" and "what" I do. I listened to Simon Sinek, and I journeyed life by capturing the title of his book, *Start With Why*. I was not willing to complain, and I was not willing to subject myself to being a future victim. I am limitless; I am a God and my "why" is tied to the God inside me, the same God (Christ) that dwelled inside Jesus. Now, it is time for me to share my limitless spirit with the world and to **return** to the world as my best version—an enhanced mind, perfected body, and evolved spirit. I share my limitless spirit through seminars, training others to be limitless; I give inspirational talks to people, inspiring them to see their limitless potential; and I write books, educating people about the power of being limitless. I was tired of losing and tired of being a loser; I am a winner, and I focus on winning. I had to **return**, so I could teach other people to win. And, I strongly believe all of us *can* win and *will* win, personally and professionally, in our limitless lives. We will never accept and embrace the roles of losers in this life, and we will forever experience life as limitless beings—freed from victimhood. We will forever get our smoke up and live the remainder of our finite experience as a badass, every second of every day, whether it is a so-called good or so-called bad encounter.

- In what ways have you played the victim?
- What can you do stop being a victim and to reclaim your role as a hero?
- What obstacle are you still struggle to overcome?

- How can you become a hero in that situation? (Paint a vivid picture and envision yourself winning.)
- Can you accept yourself as a God? Why or why not?
- Describe what it would be like to be a God for one day and do it from an unconditional loving point of view.

# Get Your Smoke Up: My 86,400 Second Rule

*"Winners focus on winning. Losers focus on winners."*
*~ Eric Thomas*

Have you ever witnessed the process of something delectable being cooked on a stove? Cooking can be a beautiful process—similar to humankind's evolution, as one's mind shifts to something of perceived greatness—when we cook and eat from a loving stance and choose to suspend all judgment. My parents cooked plenty of amazing home-cooked meals when I was a child, but I always expected that from them. However, when I first got married, my wife was not an experienced cook. Many of our dates were spent at some quick-service establishment, so I never viewed her as much of a cook. I knew she loved me, and she wanted to cook meals I preferred to eat. One time, she came home from work and suggested that she was going to fry me some chicken. I witnessed the love in her eyes, and I became filled with joy, knowing that she wanted to make me happy. She got to work, prepping and frying up some pieces of chicken, and smiling as she was generating smoke throughout our tiny apartment.

Her love was contagious, causing me to radiate unconditional vibrations of love throughout the apartment. This contagious energy spread, and it produced a deep unconditional love, where judgment could not exist. My wife's rookie days of cooking challenged her, but I enjoyed everything she cooked, because my love suspended all judgment and accepted all of her commitment and efforts. I refused to eat any fruit from the Tree of Knowledge, so I would never label her cooking as good or bad. Every piece of chicken was smothered with love and hot sauce, so it was perfect and made from her, a perfect image of God. In life, we take chances and we continuously fail, in order to be great. I have failed over a hundred times in most situations, and maybe even a thousand, in some situations. I am the master of the world's word for "sucking," but I have embraced and come to love so-called "sucking." For when I suck at something, I work even harder at that something to know that none of my accomplishments in that something came from luck. Only limited beings believe in luck because it serves as a good reason to diminish someone's effort, holding a limited mindset perspective. I promise you, we will fail multiple times during our growth process.

We all need to realize that there is no such thing as failure unless we become too immobilized to keep working and growing. People are quick to label failure as something bad rather than accepting and embracing failure as a natural part of our growth process. Dr. Carol Dweck wrote an excellent book called *Mindset*. This book highlights two types of individuals: fixed-mindset people and growth-mindset people. Individuals who operate under the rules of a fixed mindset believe they simply *are* this or that, and there is no way to change it. Growth-minded individuals believe change is inevitable, so they do not believe in failure. These individuals view failure as a necessary part of the process, so we can view fixed-minded people as limited and growth-minded as limitless. The limitless individuals become Gods, while limited individuals become godless and in need of a savior, a God to transform their lives into something that could be better than their best. The big takeaway is this: individuals who endure failure and who believe they are limitless will tap into their inner Gods and live my 86,400 second rule.

What is the 86,400 second rule? It is to take the time given every day and to make the most out of the time. We only receive 86,400 seconds every day, so we need to optimize our time with excellence.

Yet, I refer to the process of enduring failures and remaining optimistic as "Get Your Smoke Up (GYSU)." This is part of my daily routine, to tell myself:

> *"Today is a glorious day and, for 86,400 seconds, I will give my excellence and my best until I am laid to rest. I am abundantly blessed and never stressed...Check Your Life: Be Limitless."*

Victims can never GYSU because they waste precious seconds as they try to come up with reasons to define and to justify their failures. While limitless Gods view problems as reasons to innovate potential solutions, GYSU is an inner inspiration that makes us limitless. This becomes a conscious commitment to my 86,400 second rule; it becomes a belief that death is certain. We need to take this statement seriously. We will die, and we are not privy to the specific second of our exodus. When we shift our minds to this growth perspective, we will live with no guarantees, no promised tomorrows. I view my life with a commitment to personal excellence, viewing death as something glorious and pain as an illusion, a re-direction to my ultimate truth of being limitless. The truth is that all of our containers will expire. Our bodies are mortal, and we all have a temporal existence in this physical realm. Everything that breathes will cease to exist within the conceptual capacity of our humanistic minds. This is why sages and seers encourage us to walk by faith, and not by sight. We are taught what we see is real, so seeing becomes all too real. When we only believe what we see, it limits our spiritual sight and untapped powers in this physical realm. However, when we operate with limitless faith, we manifest limitless actions in our individual physical realms. Notice, limitless beings manufacture their own physical realms where they become limitless Gods.

"Faith without works is dead"[15]. I interpret this scripture as my limitless faith functions as a concomitant to my limitless actions, making my outcomes rise above any limited thinking that derives from judgments and opinions of finite beings. Many judgmental people from my milieu surmised that I would never graduate from college and never lead a so-called successful life. Some people thought I might eventually occupy a prison cell for an indiscriminate length of time. They were wrong about me, but I must admit the odds were in their favor. If verdicts are based on our factual sight, external judgment would be far superior than our internal judgment.

It is factual that I received every suspension possible while in school: in-school detention, after-school detention, Saturday school detention, and out-of-school suspension, as well as school bus suspension. I sold drugs; I ran away from home at 17 years of age; I fathered two children by two different women by 17 years of age; I dropped out of school briefly at 17 years old; and I affiliated with a dangerous gang at 19 years old. Statistically, one in every four black males have served time in prison, and black males, 16-24 years of age are more likely to be murdered in the U.S. than any other demographic[16]. Teenage fathers are more likely to engage in criminal activity and fail to graduate from high school or college. First generation college graduates have a 33% dropout rate, which is higher than college students who had a parent graduate from college. These are statistical facts, but I never subjected myself to those limitations, even when the cards were stacked against me.

I created this hell, and I subjected myself to their judgment. We subject ourselves when we tend to care about other peoples' opinions. I conjured up every negative opinion and acted on all those negative opinions. I vibrated on a negative frequency and permeated drama in my personal space to produce a hell on my personal earth. This is a perfect example that heaven and hell exist, and it is not about preparing for some external place in the afterlife. Our finite minds cannot conceptualize a life after we die, but we can conceptualize our personal earths. Our personal earths are somewhat predictive to people who choose not to take risks or who choose to limit themselves by what they choose to see. The fixed-minded or limited being tends to fear death and tends to stay in the known, so it is impossible to GYSU. We can GYSU and break free from the chains of a life where we sit and wait to have heaven in the afterlife. We limit ourselves when we wait for some better existence or expect God to pay us back for all of our shortcomings. We are the untapped Gods who subject ourselves to some perpetual heaven or hell within our limited minds. Yet, heaven and hell live in our spirits, not in some external realm. Limited beings lack the fleshly ability to think beyond their earthly temples and feel heaven. Only limitless Gods can experience an infinite life that ascends our fleshly temples. GYSU led me to dream beyond my poor decisions and to believe beyond my consequences of those poor decisions. I became limitless in my thinking, and then my thinking influenced my vibration, my vibration inspired my attitude, my attitude changed my actions, and my actions evolved into my habitual habits. Ultimately, my habits became my internal character which trumped anyone's opinions about me.

GYSU is a process that promotes positive habits, and positive habits made me an intentional limitless being. My smoke started to rise when I stopped agreeing with all of my self-imposed and self-created lies. When I stopped eating fruit from the Tree of Knowledge, all of my conditioned lies began to lose their limited power. When I chose to eat limitless fruit from the Tree of Life, I no longer accepted those lies, such as: *I am bound for prison, bound for an early death, bound for drama, and bound to attract negativity.* I rewrote my own narrative, believing and knowing instead: *I am unconditional love, I am limitless, I am all-powerful, I am God, I am heaven on earth, and I am a limitless being beyond human measure.* My given and knowledge-based narrative constructed limitations and negative beliefs while my growth and life-based narrative produced extensions and positive beliefs. The first narrative handicapped me and made me a victim who needed a savior, but the second narrative empowered me and made me a hero in my personal heaven. GYSU enables us to focus on the process of our evolutions rather than eyeing subjective outcomes of merited successes. My evolution from a consumer of fruit from the Tree of Knowledge to a consumer of fruit from the Tree of Life transformed me from a limited victim into a limitless hero.

My limitless paradigm shifted from a flawed peasant to a perfect God. I began to see my so-called imperfections as my God-given perfections; I saw only potential greatness in me. I was determined to never operate as an enemy to myself again. As I accepted myself with this new unconditional love, I started viewing pain as an illusion, and death as a glorious conclusion to my heaven on this physical earth. I understand the conflict that might exist in your minds as you all read my previous statement about pain and death. Trust me, I get it. I felt the same way as I questioned the importance of pain and the significance of death to our temporal states. The questions I asked myself were as follows:

- Why do we have pain?
- Why do some people die in horrific fashions?
- And, how can we use pain and death to serve our limitless mindsets or heavenly states?

First and foremost, pain and death are necessary conditions to our fleshly experience in this physical realm. Pain alerts us to issues in our psychological and/or physical spheres. I would argue that joy would not feel as great if we never experienced pain. I will attribute that declaration to the great rapper Curtis Jackson, also known as "50 Cent." The conundrum is most people run from pain and suppress their pain with sex, drugs, alcohol, or anything else to distract any unpleasant feeling during their fleshly experience. Pain will cease completely in sentient beings when we no longer muster up another breath on our physical planes. Life was breathed into the nostrils of us to activate our spirits[17]; and breath is the last thing expelled to deactivate our spirits. Steve Jobs called death a change agent; out with the old and in with the new.

Death is simply a glorious event, a necessary event to clear a path for the new beings to occupy this physical plane. This statement is not meant to be insensitive or heartless to readers who have lost loved ones. I understand your pain; not personally to your individual situations, but I have lost a lot of loved ones during this physical experience. I have lost countless family members and friends to murder, car accidents, and drugs; and the unsettling nature of their bodies in their deceased states was never a glorious encounter. Death is hard on the living, not the deceased; the deceased are free from the chains and conditions of this world. My reference to a glorious death is focused on our limitless spirits continuing to exist outside of our limited temples. This process causes us to GYSU, and to feel and to see beyond any pain or thoughts of impending death. Prior to a limitless way to perceive death, my finite thinking taught me to dwell on pain and to explore all potential negative outcomes of that pain. For example, I had five knee surgeries (three on the right knee and two on the left), one foot surgery, one hip surgery, and foot drop on my left leg (a damaged peroneal nerve). All of these surgeries have led me to a total hip replacement at the tender age of 39. When I was a limited victim, I complained about the pain and limited range of motion in my body. The more I played victim, the more I needed a doctor or other external influences to make me feel better about myself. As a victim, I ran from my pain, mentally and physically. But as I shifted from a victim to a hero, I embraced and found joy in my physical pain.

I utilized my pain to humble me and to bring me to a stance of gratefulness. I employed my pain to cry out, thanking God, acknowledging that all my pain is temporary. After this acknowledgement, I became grateful for my ability to use my pain to raise my awareness to other people who faced more difficult challenges. My pain was employed to pray for other people and to trust that my inner God would give me the strength to perform in theater and to run during the course of my pain. In reality, my hip hurts every day of my life, but it does not distract me from my boundless joy. I suffer daily from stabbing pain in my left side and in my left inner groin. When I feel it, it sometimes stops my walking momentum, but as I slow down, I find joy in my pain, using that joy to be grateful for pain and to be grateful for death. Gratitude made pain an illusion and death a glorious affair in my life. I am grateful every time I feel a sharp pain in my hip, as it reminds me that I have a hip to assist me in my walking endeavor. I don't see it as a hinderance, as limited-minded people might suggest.

If my knee swells and locks up, I remind myself I have feet to decrease the weight bearing on my knee. Ironically, our acceptance of physical pain builds up our resiliency to psychological pain. Pain alerts me to faulty wiring in my mind, body, and spirit. Even though I am grateful for pain, I will admit that one of the purposes of pain is to alert us to more serious issues within our minds, bodies, and spirits. I still visit dentists and medical doctors for ailments that impede my reason for existing on this planet. In the summer of 2009, I had severe stomach pains and feared it might be potentially cancerous. I was vomiting blood, and the pain immobilized me at times. My mind went to the extreme, and my spirit felt weak, as fear consumed me and spread throughout my mind, body, and spirit. I decided to let go and let God, recognizing my fear could never improve my current condition. I went on with my life as normal, and I stopped telling people about my pain. I stopped throwing pity parties (external motivation) to improve my psychological emotions; instead, I used my limitless spirit (internal motivation) to give me the psychological strength.

I became grateful for the stomach pain and utilized it to refocus my life's perspective, becoming aware that life is temporary and that I do will not be able to live forever. I witnessed the unlimited value of time, and the limitless beauty found in every precious second of time. Most people perceive time as a linear or mathematical ray, consisting of a starting point that leads along a directional arrow somewhere forward. The issue is this: our starting points represent the past, and our arrows represent the unknown or our futures. Our pasts and our futures do not exist, so we must abandon this concept of time if we aim to remain limitless. My adoption of infinite time led me to live in the here and the *now*, which provided me with the gratitude needed to value every second and to remain neutral of pain, joy, and death. When we live in this reality, we understand our expectations of equality or expectations of anything can produce a world of suffering. Limitless Gods raise their personal **B.A.R.** (we'll dig more into this in the next chapter), so they can *be* the change, instead of waiting for the world to change. When we change, our perception of time becomes infinite. Time becomes a limitless richness of wealth, and time is transformed into an open circle, with no boundaries and no points to produce any measures of finite time. Limitless beings stop seeing time as a second, a minute, an hour, or a day; they simply see time as *now*. I GYSU every morning by using my following 86,400 second rule to keep me in the state of *now* throughout every second:

*Today is a glorious day and, for 86,400 seconds, I will give my excellence and my best until I am laid to rest. I am abundantly blessed and never stressed...Check Your Life: Be Limitless.*

- What are you attempting to generate energy to overcome?
- How can you GYSU in every second?
- What do you do to be mindful in every second?
- What pain ails you?
- How can you use that pain to be grateful?
- What power comes from this place of gratefulness?

# My Charge to You Sentient Beings: Raise Your Personal B.A.R.

*"I don't think the dreams die – I think that people give up. I think it gets too hard."*
*~ Tyler Perry*

The aim of this book is to challenge all of us to take charge of our individual lives, so that we can make our personal earths and our personal heavens permanent during our physical existence. At this point in our book, yes, *our* book, we should all be vibrating on the same high and positive frequency of unconditional love. A limitless belief and love that conquers all impossible obstacles in this conditioned world. What is the most seemingly impossible obstacle in this conditioned world? It is to love yourself and your fellow human beings beyond any manmade labels and to stop consuming conceptual lies from the Tree of Knowledge.

We must move beyond our conditioned ways of thinking because most conditioning is not designed to benefit us or to serve our limitless beings. Conditioning is constructed to build order and to create an agreement with societal norms. Norms are employed to produce some sense of perceived normalcy in the collective ego of our respectable societies. In order to build our heavens in our personal earths, we must be willing to repudiate most of our conditions and manmade labels. This requires a debunking of our old traditions, and in some situations, it demands crazy faith, a faith in esoteric knowledge, the unseen. A faith that challenges the uncomfortable attitudes and beliefs of our parents, friends, religious leaders, and societal norms. This is so challenging because most people do not have a desire to offend our loved ones, friends, and respected citizens. It is imperative to depart from negativity and to cut dead weight as we raise our personal **B.A.R.** (**B.A.R.** stands for **belief, aim**, and **receive**) and attempt to transition to our limitless existence.

We, the sentient beings, need everybody's untapped gifts. We need the purity of our gifts, the inner truth or motivation that drives all of our gifts. The truth and limitlessness of our gifts can only be shared when we decide to experience life, by consuming fruit from the Tree of Life and by sharing our gifts and awesomeness in every second of the *now*. My charge requires immediate and constant commitment to the *now*; we must stop looking behind to the past and stop jumping too far ahead to the future. We entered the physical realm with inherited gifts, and we were all charged to share those gifts with this world. We are required to raise our personal **B.A.R.** if we intend to sustain our limitlessness and God state.

- **B. Belief** demands us to have faith in the unseen, knowing that esoteric energies, spirits, or God, are working in favor on our behalf. In order for us to tap into our inner belief, we must be able to selfishly love ourselves in an unconditional manner. When we are able to love in this fashion, we will be able to believe beyond our conditional beliefs; beyond the belief of seeing with our eyes rather than our hearts. Faith lies deep in our hearts, and our hearts enable us to express our inner truths from our spirits. Our hearts are the keys to unlocking all doors to living in the present moment.

- **A.** When we **aim** in the present, we put a rocket of desire out into the universe for some unknown time period in the future. The power of this position and the act is that it creates a dream state in our conscious minds. This is where we develop the so-called beautiful mind and produce lofty dreams in our personal heavens. In this mind, my heaven was birthed and lived in a corporeal fashion. This is where my dream of playing professional football was born; this is where I overcame a life of crime; this is where I wrote my first book; this is where I saw my first acting role; this is where I earned my PhD; this is where I made tenure; this is where I made millions of dollars; this is where I created a beautiful marriage and family; this is where I lost 55 pounds; this is where I no longer had to take blood pressure medication; and this is where I became a limitless God. I aimed to be more than a mere man or a limited being. I aimed to be limitless, and I wanted to live out all of my uniqueness. I realized there was only one me, and I was the only one born to fulfill a very specific purpose, a purpose only gifted to me.

I understand it is extremely difficult for religious people to buy into the concept of being a limitless God because most religions program us to find God outside of ourselves. I believe religion is a beautiful thing; religion pointed me to a belief in God. However, all religions are manmade. It was challenging for me to accept the flawed system of religions because I was a boy who grew up in the Baptist church, where I faithfully served as an usher and as a choir member. I felt like God was watching me and judging me for everything I did incorrectly, making it difficult for me to love my life and to love others. **Aim** became possible for me when I no longer consumed those lies from a manmade religion. Personally, I admired what internally motivated

Jesus (Christ), Mohammed, and Buddha, to share unconditional love in this world and to make this world better for
other sentient beings. These seers were beautiful souls, and
their internal motivation made them limitless. Finite beings tainted their spiritual messages when they made spiritual messages specific to their religious practices; and those
same finite beings used their religion to make them superior to other beings and religions practiced in our vast
world.

Galatians 3:27 says, "for all of you who were baptized into
Christ have clothed yourselves with Christ." This means
that those who believe in Christ also embody the spirit of
Christ. Galatians 3:28 adds, "There is neither Jew nor Gen-
tile, neither slave nor free, nor is there male and female,
for you are all one in Christ Jesus." If we are all one in
Christ, who was considered God in the human form, according to Christian doctrine? Why is it so hard for most
Christians to view themselves as God in a unified and unconditional loving spirit? We must **aim** to be higher than
our given physical forms, which are considered limited by
most human beings. My **aim** placed my mind and my spirit
into an esoteric realm of possibility, a spiritual peace where
all things were possible. I was not put on this earth to be
the greatest running back in football or some short-sen-
sational basketball player, as I thought as an unconscious
child. Football and basketball are manmade creations, and
personally, manmade creations made me focus on external
jobs rather than my internal purpose. This thinking limited
me from seeing expansive possibilities and infinite opportunities for my life. Even if I was chosen to play football at
the highest level, my gift would have emerged as a speaker,

an entertainer, or anything that inspired people to reach deeper within to their limitless God. I was not put on this earth to play sports as a limitless being.

- **R.** This takes me to my last charge within this power process, to **receive**. To **receive** means mentally and spiritually taking what we **believe**, and what we **aim** for in our limitless, God-conscious state. When we inject ourselves into the **receive** state, we abandon all our worries and journey down an all-knowing path—not all-expecting, but all-*knowing*. Being all-knowing inspires me to walk in a constructed heaven with all those things, relationships, and places I believed in and aimed for. This is where we become Gods, this is where we remain limitless, and this is where we receive all manna (e.g., blessings from the spirit world) to sustain our God-conscious and limitless spirits. If we expect things, relationships, and places to come into existence, we assemble potential suffering in our lives, as Buddha suggests. Buddha stated, "Peace begins when expectations end." Buddha encouraged acceptance and urged us to break attachments to people because attachments create expectations that lead to suffering. When I died to expectations and embraced the knowing, I no longer became frazzled when some of my dreams failed to come to fruition. I knew I would play professional football when I exited the military in August of 2003; however, I did not sign a professional football contract until January of 2005, with the Raleigh Rebels, in Raleigh, NC. The Raleigh Rebels came as a new arena football team to capture the former Carolina Cobras fanbase. Prior to signing with the Raleigh Rebels, I was rejected by the Fayetteville Patriots in 2003 and was left dejected by multiple professional football workouts during those two years of training and believing: one team in Greensboro, NC, one in Atlanta, GA, and one in Raleigh, NC. I trained three times a day. I was grateful for the opportunity to train and to work out with professional clubs, but I did not expect anything from those tryouts. I had no attachments to the outcomes because I envisioned myself playing football again somewhere; I just did not know where it would be or when it would come to fruition. I developed an unconditional love for the workout process while training with powerlifters and sprinting with former football players at a high school track and field facility. I developed the best mind, body, and spirit while attempting to play professional football. I deliberately aimed for something that seemed impossible by my military family and immediate family members, and the more they doubted the process, the more I believed in my intuition. I was not attached to their beliefs and not conditioned to their eye-tested realities; my mind envisioned myself smiling and signing a contract as coaches waited for my signature, and making long touchdown runs up the field. I became limitless, and this experience propelled me to a God-state of believing the unbelievable, ascending to a level of limitlessness where I could receive the impossible. Raising my personal **B.A.R.** has led me to play professional football after six years removed from college football and to start for one season, scoring a 28-yard touchdown run in the playoffs against the Canton Legends from Canton, OH.

This accomplishment led me to mental, spiritual, and physical wealth, which also led me to acquire many worldly successes. I believed if I could propel my body to play at that level, I could propel my mind to think at an even greater level. My personal successes are seen as something special to some people in the outside world because many people conceptualize limitations in their own lives, not realizing my successes are their successes. I believe everyone has the potential to do what I do and even greater, when they remain true to their authentic purpose. Most people do not believe in being limitless, and most people struggle with the acceptance of being a God. If we only knew about our true limitless potential, we would understand that worldly successes come as signposts from the universe or the ultimate source of all energy. Signposts normally inform us that we are tapping into our limitless potential and using our gifts to serve our greater purpose. Our successes should inspire others rather than becoming accolades to validate and to feed our Godless E.G.O.s. Remember, the more we feed, the more we edge God out of our lives and temporary situations.

We must become mindful to stay in our present moments. We must also fall in unconditional love with the process of raising our personal **B.A.R.**, so we can eliminate any attachments to our worldly successes. I charge all sentient beings to utilize our energies to shine brightly, by experiencing life and quelling all judgment of other things and people. How do we experience life and stop all judgment? Confucius stated, "Silence is a true friend who never betrays." In order to transform our limited beings into Gods, we must stop unconsciously talking and consuming fruit from the Tree of Knowledge, and we must start consciously listening and consuming fruit from the Tree of Life. "Then the Lord God said, 'Look, the human beings have become like us, knowing both good and evil. What if they reach out, take fruit from the tree of life, and eat it? Then they will live forever!'"[18].

- Do you believe it is possible to eat fruit from the Tree of Life and live forever?
- How can you consume the proper fruit *now*?
- Why do you want to wait to die to experience heaven?
- How can you raise your personal **B.A.R.** to experience heaven on earth?

# Check Your Life: Be Limitless...Practical Usage in My Life

*"The most important thing is to try and inspire people so that they can be great in whatever they want to do."*
*- Kobe Bryant*

The universe was always working on my behalf, even during the so-called bad moments. I intensely believe the same is true for you, no matter your current situation; and once again, I am not writing this to disparage your past or current situations. I only write to inspire, so we can witness the foundational power that rests inside all of us. I have compassion for all of your situations...I do, and I understand your situations might bring about some real fear for you. However, if you are reading my words, it is something so deep and powerful inside of you that can lift you above all your situations; and I believe you are at this point in our book because you truly believe it. I will leave you with one last governing statement before I proceed to discuss the usage of "Check Your Life: Be Limitless" in my personal life.

We are all mortals in the physical realm, and the very best part of us will leave our finite bodies, meaning nothing in this realm can ever touch our God or inner spirit. I was told by some loved ones as an adolescent that I was stupid, ugly, and a failure. Even some of my school administrators and teachers told me I would probably end up in prison one day. Some pastors and religious figures believed I was destined for a place in hell. Remember, all truth begins with a question. What do they know about the inherent me? What do I even know about the inherent me? The answer to both questions was nothing.

Our truths are our origins, and our origins are what we were prior to embarking on this human experience and prior to placing the best part of us in our vessels, our Gods. This is the proper fruit from the Tree of Life and not the lies told to us as innocent kids when we unknowingly ate conditioned fruit from the Tree of Knowledge. We are never truly fulfilled when we measure this experience with what we know, because there will always be more to learn and know. I accepted these understandings as the truth, and it became my gospel and holy grail. When people spoke ill of me, it offended me and sometimes I acted according to the labels (e.g., skipping class and school) applied to my life. I started living their subjective beliefs about me and suppressed my limitless potential; but the universe was always working on my behalf. My constant infractions in school and my anger issues at home prompted my mother to register me for a play called *Cowboy Capers*. This play was directed by the late great Bob Johnson. Bob would encourage me to connect with the audience, to smile, to have fun, and to never be afraid of the audience. He built my confidence, and he taught me to harness my discomfort on the stage into something beautiful and limitless.

This limitless gift was that the audience was waiting to witness the love and best parts of me. At this time, I did not have a desire to act, to teach, or to participate in theatre; but now, I get paid very well to do all three. I was actually uncomfortable with all of those activities, as well as writing. The universe was always working on my behalf. I fought a lot of people, verbally and physically. I was very competitive by nature and showed minimal compassion at times, so I pursued a winning-mentality—at all costs in sports and in random situations. My robust demeanor and aggressive nature led to constant trouble, but my constant trouble led to additional opportunities for me. For instance, my teachers made me write about my emotions and "why" I acted out in class, they forced me to sit quietly in timeout to reflect on my actions, and they made me get up in front of the class to discuss how I would improve my classroom behavior. All the while, my parents continued to force me to act in stage plays and in church plays. I was also told that God lives in me, so I need to emulate the scriptures rather than read the scriptures. I learned to *do* rather than simply say what I was going do. Once again, the universe was always working on my behalf.

My faults and poor decision-making kept giving me disciplined opportunities to grow, as a writer, as a speaker, and as an actor. These opportunities also began to fortify my confidence, developing a high level of self-efficacy as a performer. Bob Johnson, our play director, encouraged me to take command of the stage and to realize the audience is here for me; I learned it was my job to serve them and to give them a memorable performance when I was on stage—always, no short-cuts to giving my best performance. Truth be told, I hated speaking, writing, and acting in elementary school; but the universe knew my destiny, my purpose, and it was determined to guide me toward my innate gifts and limitless path. When I sat in timeout, I daydreamed and shifted my mind to a world of optimistic beliefs—a vast world of something better. Also, my infractions led to states of mindfulness when I cogitated over my actions and devised better solutions and ways to be better than my best. I created a world where I was king; I was God. I ruled over my intimate domain, and there were no finite rules to limit my unharnessed potential. In this world, I possessed the ability to rise above school suspensions, selling drugs, being a womanizer and a violent individual, and any other prescribed labels. I was label-less and boundless of worldly opinions.

"Check Your Life: Be Limitless" was born out of all my disfunc-
tion, which redirected me to mindfulness and believing in my limitless alternatives. In August of 1999, I chose life and a world with
no labels. James Williams began to die to me, and all associated ti-
tles died with that birth-given name. I was no longer J-Roc, a football player, a thug, or anything assigned to me. Mentally, I believed
it was all a lie—even my blackness, my maleness, and anything-ness
tied to the God in me. I decided to stop playing life with a game
of categories because it created confusion; and God is not the author of confusion[19]. I strongly began to believe God was in me, so I
was above all of the worldly games and categories. I surmised that
my vessel was here, but my spirit dwelled and generated power from
an esoteric realm far from this world I occupied. I wrote down my
dreams and goals on a piece a paper to get them out of my mind,
but as the dreams gained some smoke, I wrote them more vividly.
The more vivid the dream, the more I knew that it was an authentic
dream that would eventually manifest in my physical world. "Check
Your Life: Be Limitless" brought all these dreams to fruition in my
meaningless life. All physical lives are meaningless; it is our spiritual
lives that have meaning. The most significant dream on my list was
realized when I asked the universe for my wife in January of 2000,
and she agreed to marry me on February 8, 2000, one month after a
serious courtship.

My union ignited a snowball effect. Positive opportunities created additional opportunities, and they started to roll and accumulate in abundance. I told the universe I would give it my life if it
allowed me to marry my wife. Ever since then, I have been serving
the universe or God with my innate gifts and limitless being. I became "Airman of the Year" at Holloman AFB, NM in 2002 and won
an incentive flight on a T-38 training jet. That unexpected and appreciated opportunity inspired me to pursue a professional career
in football after I separated from the military, in July of 2003. As I

pursued that bold dream, life continued to kick back and to put difficult obstacles on my path. One time, I begged and pleaded with the social security commission welfare officers for assistance, but I was turned away and laughed at by some of those welfare agents. In my time of need, I was quickly turned away. I needed money for food and to pay for other miscellaneous bills, so I decided to pursue a master's degree to receive GIBILL benefits—money for school and additional money for bills. Once again, the universe was working on my behalf.

I got a job working for BB&T because I wanted to move into management. However, my supervisor kept blocking my request and eventually, she found a way to terminate me from my fraudulent specialist position. I was humbled by her decision, as I walked past our appointed security officer and former co-workers, as I tightly clutched the brown box that included my Bob Marley CD, my radio, my Bible, and my half-used crossword puzzle book, exiting that building never to return. This was a surreal and humbling experience for a former Airman of the Year in the United States Air Force. It was obvious that my supervisor was determined to terminate me. But she did not realize, what she intended for harm raised my awareness to other career opportunities and a limitless outlook. I began to question my career path and my purpose, knowing immediately that it was not to pursue a management position in the banking industry. I explored the idea of inspiring others as an educator and as an abstract thinker. The universe was still working on my behalf. During this time, I taught some adjunct classes in the Management department at Wilson Technical Community college, but I yearned for more. When I taught management classes, my passion seemed to come alive and my actions felt natural as I sauntered around the classroom.

Yet, I decided to take a leadership job as a department supervisor at Stock Building Supply. I was proud to hire, to train, and to attempt to sustain talented employees for the largest door distributor in the South. I proudly led a talented group of 61 people. We were responsible for producing and shipping interior doors for residential properties. I realized my joy came from motivating and inspiring my teammates to pursue dreams that expanded beyond our production floor rather than driving them to work themselves to the bone. I saw my teammates as more than proverbial employees. I viewed them as equals, and individuals with limitless potential. However, some individuals saw them as numbers and human machinery. My leadership style clashed with management, as I was informed to terminate a worker whom I viewed as a quality team member. This quelled my desire to stay in manufacturing and business operations, so I sought a job in education, at a secondary school. I worked for the next four years as a business instructor, computer applications instructor, keyboarding instructor, and algebra instructor. This was not my intended path, but it was my given path. My stint as an educator guided me to pursue my doctorate degree, to meet Chris Roberts (a mentor), and to enter higher education as a professor. Between those years, I played two years of professional arena football, only to realize it was never about playing professional football.

Arena football demonstrated my passion for inspiring others. I fell in love with conversing with fans after our games and motivating them to reach for their limitless dreams. Since then, I have traversed the world, speaking and teaching in Spain, France, South Korea, China, Bulgaria, and all throughout the U.S. I have acted in television shows, commercials, one movie, and one animated film. I also performed in multiple touring plays (e.g., *Jackie Robinson*) and executed voice-overs for local commercials. I delivered a TED Talk and wrote multiple books. Personally, I have acquired many worldly successes over the past two decades, but I realized that these so-called successes or multiple vocations never defined me or fulfilled me. Life is meaningless when we make it about so-called external successes. None of those external successes highlighted my inner gifts. My inner gifts endowed me with abilities to perform my past and current vocations and to acquire those worldly successes while being able to enjoy the process—not the destination.

My inner gifts brought life to my external gifts. If this sounds confusing, we must remember our inner gift is our intuitive nature (internal DNA), and our outer gifts are our reactive and proactive nature (external DNA). One of my external gifts was my prowess to speak and to speak with an intuitive passion and sense of knowing—unconditional love delivered from my intuitive nature. I speak with veracity and inspiration because I feel the truth deep inside of me and that truth stirs up my limitless power. That is how I serve the world, these are my ultimate gifts: to believe, to receive, to speak, to act, and to write with an expression of unconditional love. Gifts that enable me to live a limitless and God-inspired life, so others can feel the positive vibrations and be inspired to live limitless lives as well. When this spirit is birthed in us, we will attract many successes and a plethora of additional opportunities tied to our authentic paths.

"Check Your Life: Be Limitless" guided me to one moment, and I saw life in the following practical manner. A lot of people are willing to sell their souls and even demean themselves to acquire a quick dollar or some external successes. Yet, we should consider this subsequent scenario:

> *Imagine if every day we wake up, we were given $86,400 from the rulers of this world. The only caveat is that we must spend all of this money prior to the conclusion of any 24-hour period, in any given day. None of the money can be saved for another day, it must all used to acquire things for that specific day. What would you do? Would you wake up earlier? Would you*

*take more calculated risks? Would you find unique ways to maximize every dollar? When I present this scenario to most people, they describe how they would use every dollar. They brag about how they would enjoy spending every dollar and brag about how they would get the most out of every day. Some people even describe how they would be willing to wake up early, so they can jump start their day. They boast about how they would maximize every second—every second. The beauty of this scenario is that many of these people get excited and smile as they plan out their day.*

The reality is...money is a resource...that's it—nothing more and nothing less. A resource that provides us with opportunities to invest and to procure items and purchases in this world. Outside of these usages of money, money is worthless. However, it has the power to inspire people to work, to rob, to steal, and to kill other people for it. The love of money is the root of all evil, but big corporations, parents, and people make sure to teach each other to love it. Most people do it in seemingly harmless ways, by encouraging their kids to be doctors and engineers, so they can make a lot of money and to have a stable life. We teach people to seek a career for money rather than to seek a career for fulfillment or enjoyment; so subconsciously, we are teaching people to love money. What if we taught kids to eat fruit from the Tree of Life and to love themselves; what if we never spoke of money? Do we trust that the universe would bring money to honor their inherent truth and their inherent love? The universe or God only gives us 86,400 seconds in a given day to spend our time wisely. It is imperative for us to understand that our seconds are more precious and more valuable than any amount of money we will ever receive in the physical realm. We must be inspired by this statement, and we must be determined to use our remaining time to inspire us and to move us to a limitless position.

This is the only state I know, and it is the only state I will accept until I can breathe no more. I will conclude our book with the following declarations. I am limitless, I am perfection, and I am a God. You are limitless, you are perfection, and you are a God. When you wake up in the morning, you need to look at yourself beyond your physical form and recognize the perfect spirit that made you. Remember to walk by faith and not by sight[20]. Now say this to yourself every morning and throughout each glorious day:

*Today is a glorious day and for 86,400 seconds, I will give my excellence and my best until I am laid to rest. I am abundantly blessed and never stressed...Check Your Life: Be Limitless.*

# *Epilogue*

On December 7$^{th}$, 2019, I landed in Shanghai, China. The next morning, I met my friend Joy in the hotel lobby, so we could catch our flight to Xiamen. We casually discussed my mindfulness workshop that I planned to present at the regional Wuhan conference. Joy asked me if I had seen *Frozen 2*, and I told her I hadn't yet, but I wanted to watch it with my daughter, Jocelyn, who was 11 at the time. Immediately, she suggested that it was an absolute must-watch movie. She said the biggest takeaway was that when we do not know what to do next, we need to simply do "the next right thing."

This message resonated with my spirit on many mental and spiritual levels, and it led me to pursue intentional righteousness as I prepared to educate my Chinese brothers and sisters in Wuhan. When I spoke on December 14$^{th}$ in Wuhan, my spirit wanted me to deliver a message beyond my simple educational tactics, enabling me to encourage them to be authentic and to be more than a proverbial college professor. I spoke hope, and I introduced them to a concept that I coined, "A.N.D." which stands for Awareness, No judgment, and Do excellence. Someone asked me, "What would you do if you were threatened with termination for doing the right thing in the classroom but the right thing went against school policy?"

I stated that it is always best to do the next right thing, even if my administration decided to terminate me. Someone said, "But, we need to make money to survive." I said, "You are correct, if your intention is only to survive." When we are limitless, we thrive and move beyond those psychological fears of just trying to survive. I told them that all our fears require A.N.D. as our rebuttal. I spoke this message from the depths of my soul and from a rich veracity that came from the purest part of my spirit. This message was for them, but it ended up being a message that inspired me to be more hopeful, as an individual and as a collective member of my society. I left Wuhan on December 15th to head back to Shanghai. As I prepared to fly back to the U.S., I woke up the following morning on December 16th and stated that 2020 would be the best year of my life. On my 15-hour flight from Shanghai, China to Atlanta, GA, I was working on this book and checking my life. Yet, between my writing, I envisioned turning 40, being debt-free, embracing loving relationships, watching my son graduate from high school, making tenure, marketing and selling this book, acting in various shows, and turning my book *From Thug to Scholar* into a movie or TV deal.

I had no doubt my life was headed for a higher level. On December 31st, one day prior to the start of 2020, the Year of the Rat—which is considered the year of new experiences—Wuhan government announced that a new virus had been identified and had impacted their citizens. This new virus had no known cure. At the time, I did not pay much attention to this new virus. I believed it was contained and was no real threat to anybody outside of Wuhan, and I definitely did not believe it would impact the U.S. Well, this virus continued to spread, and on March 17th, there were confirmed cases in all 50 states throughout the U.S. As of May 31st and as I conclude this manuscript, this new virus, the coronavirus or COVID-19, is considered a pandemic and has now become an official global issue. This virus has impacted millions of lives—physically, psychologically, financially, and socially. Today our world looks vastly different, and the virus has changed our world in myriad ways. Some people are scared to shake hands, to speak to one another, and to gather in large groups. Many people have been victimized due to their ethnicity, socio-economic level, or other assigned roles. I share this continuation of Check Your Life to inform you that this is still the best year of my life, and it is still the best year of your life.

We are still breathing and pumping life through our beings; we are limitless beings beyond the scope of our limited imaginations. Limitless beings find contentment within every second and extrapolate joy from those precious seconds. Personally, this COVID-19 situation has halted my consulting jobs, impacted my son's graduation, destroyed my social interactions, and changed my teaching pedagogy, to name a few changes. "A.N.D." my complaints or my life interruptions are not that serious when compared to the seriousness of this virus and its devasting impact. I am aware that many people have fallen ill or succumbed to this deadly virus. I am aware that this virus has negatively impacted many businesses and household incomes. I am aware that this unpredictable event is just a part of life, and this event needs to be embraced and accepted like any favorable events that occur in my life. I am also aware that this virus has inspired me to slow down and to appreciate simple events, like taking a walk and listening to birds sing, as they fly from tree branch to power lines. I have no judgment about the coronavirus, and this paradigm has provided me with a clear vision to recognize unseen opportunities. I learned to value the use of Zoom to instruct my classes and to communicate with other professionals; I educated myself on the stock market; and I created new ways to work out without a gym membership. I found innovative ways to cut my own hair and to treat my growing facial hair. Without judgment, I have found a deep liberation and peace that incites me to try new things and to take calculated risks.

Finally, I have implemented my powerful mantra, do excellence. When I was complaining about not being able to go on vacations, I went on hikes and walks with my family. This was a way that I chose to do excellence. As a family, we turned simple undertakings and opportunities into marvelous adventures. Remember, we are limitless spirits, and we have excellence permanently etched in our spiritual DNAs. We come from a universal love that is absolute, making us infinite Gods in our spirits. The year 2020 is associated with the metal element, and this metal element indicates success. More specifically, the metal element is characterized as being strong, determination, and resolve. Meaning, we have no quit in us as a society and collective spirit, and we are bound to overcome this virus as one limitless spirit. The question is...how do we become the cure for the limited beings? The answer is...we must raise our awareness and recognize the need for our limitless understanding and acceptance, withhold judgment from other people or their temporary situations and meet them with unconditional love, and do excellence with every word being uttered from our mouths and every intentional interaction.

*Check Your Life: Be Limitless...Don't just give words, "be" the words "I" give.*

# Sources of Inspiration for this Book

1. Bureau of Justice Statistics. (2020). Retrieved from www.bjs.gov
2. Campbell, J. (2014). *The hero's journey: Joseph Campbell on his life and work (The collected works of Joseph Campbell) 3rd edition.* Novato, CA: New World Library.
3. Cicero, M. T. (2019). *How to think about God: An ancient guide for believers and nonbelievers.* Princeton, NJ: Princeton University Press.
4. Dyer, Wayne (2019). *Happiness is the way.* Carlsbad, CA: Hay House Publishing.
5. Goggins, D. (2018). *Can't hurt me: Master your mind and defy the odds.* Austin, TX: Lioncrest Publishing.
6. Hacker. (2019). In *Merriam-Webster.com.* Retrieved from https://www.merriam-webster.com/help/citing-the-dictionary.
7. Hicks, E., & Hicks, J. (2007). *The amazing power of deliberate intent.* Carlsbad, CA: Hay House Publishing.
8. Holiday, R. (2016). *EGO is the enemy: The fight to master our greatest opponent.* USA: Portfolio Penguin Random House Publishing.
9. Irwin, N. (2017). Priming the pump: The economic metaphor Trump 'came up with.' *The New York Times.* Retrieved from https://www.nytimes.com/2017/05/11/upshot/

priming-the-pump-the-economic-metaphor-trump-thinks-he-invented.html.

10. Jung, C. G. (2006). *The undiscovered self*. New York, NY: Signet Classics Publishing.

11. Rohr, R. (2019). *The universal Christ: How a forgotten reality can change everything we see, hope for and believe*. New York, NY: Convergent Books.

12. Ruiz, M., & Mills, J. (2004). *The voice of knowledge: A practical guide to inner peace*. San Rafael, CA: Amber-Allen Publishing.

13. Ruiz, M. (2002). *The mastery of love: A Practical guide to the art of relationship—Toltec wisdom book*. San Rafael, CA: Amber-Allen Publishing.

14. Ruiz, M. Jr. (2016). *The mastery of self: A toltec guide to personal freedom*. San Rafael, CA: Amber-Allen Publishing.

15. Seligman, M. (2011). *Flourish: A visionary new understanding of happiness and well-being*. Tampa, FL: Free Press Publishing.

16. Sinek, S. (2009). *Start with why: How great leaders inspire everyone to take action*. USA: Portfolio Penguin Random House Publishing.

17. Williams, J. A. (2020). *From thug to scholar: An odyssey to unmask my true potential*. Knoxville, TN: UnmaskYTP Publishing.

18. Zukaw, G. (2012). *The seat of the soul*. New York, NY: Simon & Schuster Publishing.

# Footnotes

1.  ^ Genesis 3:11
2.  ^ John 14:12 NIV
3.  ^ Quran 14:7
4.  ^ Lao-tzu, trans., 2000, chap. 58
5.  ^ John 8:7 NIV
6.  ^ John 8:11 NIV
7.  ^ Mark 5:34 NIV
8.  ^ Genesis 3:22 NIV
9.  ^ Jeremiah 29:11 NIV
10. ^ Genesis 1:26
11. ^ Matthew 6:30 NIV
12. ^ John 10:10 NIV
13. ^ Matthew 22:36-40 NIV
14. ^ Luke 23:34 NIV
15. ^ James 2:26 NIV
16. ^ www.bjs.gov
17. ^ Genesis 2:7 NIV
18. ^ Genesis 3:22
19. ^ 1 Corinthians 14:33
20. ^ 2 Corinthians 5:7

## ALSO BY DR. JAMES ARTHUR WILLIAMS

*From Thug to Scholar: An Odyssey to Unmask My True Potential*

*From Flab to Abs*

*UnmaskYTP Workbook*

*Let's Talk Some Leadership (Coming Soon)*

 Currently, Dr. Williams serves as an associate professor (tenured) at the University of Tennessee and is the owner of UNMASKYTP, LLC, training domestic and international leaders to dwell in joy while seeking curiosity in every endeavor. He teaches mindfulness, various leadership tactics, and one-on-one coaching to build brighter leaders for the future. He has worked with leaders in Spain, South Korea, Bulgaria, China, and at many Fortune 100 companies.

Dr. Williams is also a professional actor, performing as Uncle Tom in *Into the Wilderness (SAG/movie)* and starring as Waco Collins in *Murder Chose Me*. He wrote two books, *From Thug to Scholar: An Odyssey to Unmask my True Potential* and *How to Get Abs like a Bodybuilder but Eat like a Fat boy*. He has also published over 15 scholarly articles and delivered over 30 presentations on emotional intelligence, soft skills, sports, leadership, employee training, mentorship, hospitality pedagogy, human resource management, and personal and professional development.

Dr. Williams grew up masked, selling drugs at 13 years of age, fathering two kids, dropping out high school, and living on the streets by 17 years old.

Dr. Williams earned six degrees (two doctorates), Ph.D. from Iowa State University. He honorably served the United States Air Force, winning Airman of the Year. He played professional arena football for the Raleigh Rebels (2005-2006). Dr. Williams has industry experience in the dental, banking, sales, pharmaceuticals, manufacturing, hotels, and education. He is also a *Certified Hospitality Educator and trainer.*

Dr. Williams has also spoke to over 100 unique audiences, and won numerous speech competitions for *Toastmaster's International*; served as a keynote speaker for Coffeewood Correctional Institution, public schools, colleges, fortune 500 companies, professional organizations. Dr. Williams was also recognized as a *Top 15 Emerging Scholar of 2019* by Diverse: Issues in Higher Education. Dr. Williams also was a featured speaker for TEDx UTK in 2019. Best international mentor for Chinese Hospitality Education Initiative for the 2019 national championship in Shanghai, China.

CPSIA information can be obtained
at www.ICGtesting.com
Printed in the USA
LVHW071156200720
661030LV00010B/390